POEMS, LETTERS, AND
MEMORIES OF PHILIP SIDNEY NAIRN

P. S. F. NAIRN IN 1907.

POEMS, LETTERS, AND MEMORIES
OF PHILIP SIDNEY NAIRN

ARRANGED BY

E. R. EDDISON
Late of Trinity College, Oxford

HarperCollins*Publishers*

HarperCollins*Publishers*
77-85 Fulham Palace Road
Hammersmith, London W6 8JB
www.harpercollins.co.uk

Paperback edition published in 2014

First published in hardback for private circulation by
E. R. Eddison, London, 1916

ISBN 978-0-00-757807-8

MIX
Paper from
responsible sources
FSC C007454

FSC™ is a non-profit international organisation established to promote
the responsible management of the world's forests. Products carrying the
FSC label are independently certified to assure consumers that they come
from forests that are managed to meet the social, economic and
ecological needs of present and future generations,
and other controlled sources.

Fir

PREFACE

THE verses which form the original and essential part of this book are somewhat overshadowed in bulk by the introductory Memoir. The justification of this (to my mind a complete justification) is that it is due not (at least I hope not) to prolixity on the part of the editor, but to the inclusion of long quotations from Nairn's letters and from his diary. Some of the poems are undoubtedly worthy, in themselves and for their own sake, to be preserved. But their author wrote himself down less vividly and unmistakably in these essays in finished art than in his less studied writings, and any lasting value possessed by this compilation will, in my opinion, rest chiefly on such success as it may have in snatching from oblivion some living traits of a personality which has far more than a personal interest.

Of the defects of my share in the book I am painfully aware. It has been written in time of war, on Sundays or on late evenings, in such moments of leisure as could be found amid urgent official duties. In more favourable circumstances the area of correspondence covered might have been widened, and the balance of the whole better adjusted.

In my estimate of Nairn's character I do not pretend to be judicial. I have, however, kept a watchful eye on the pardonable leanings of a friend's judgment towards mere eulogy. I have made no statement which has not been weighed, nor any which I do not believe to be true.

I desire to thank my friend Mr. Henry Nairn for the compliment he has paid me in asking me to undertake this work, and for the assistance and information which he has ungrudgingly placed at my disposal. Also my old friend Captain M. H. Woods, for permitting me to take his name in vain. For the local and historical particulars of Kelantan I am chiefly indebted to Mr. W. A. Graham's book, which is, I believe, still the chief authority on that State. I must finally record my obligations to the Editors of the *Pall Mall Gazette* and the *Malay Mail,* who have kindly consented to the reproduction of poems which appeared originally in their publications. Two sonnets, *Exile* and *In the Buchheide,* appeared in the *Pall Mall Magazine,* now incorporated with *Nash's Magazine.* Finally, it may be noted of the pictures that Nairn appears in all of them.

E. R. E.

November, 1915.

CONTENTS

CONTENTS

POEMS

CONTENTS

LIST OF ILLUSTRATIONS

POEMS, LETTERS, AND MEMORIES
OF PHILIP SIDNEY NAIRN

CHAPTER I

INTRODUCTION

THERE are men and women of such vitality of spirit, in whom the roots of thought, of action, and of affection seem so firmly set, so safely and naturally engrafted on those abiding principles of reason, efficiency, and goodness which are the starting-point and the goal of all sane philosophy, that the mere calling of them to mind seems to question the finality of death. The barriers of the grave at the passage of such souls, put off, after the first bitterness of sorrow, their irrefragable and inexorable darkness, shrinking to a reality more tolerable and more transient; as, in Meredith's romance, the palace of Rabesqurat, Mistress of Illusions, was dissipated in the light of the Lily. This instinctive sense of death as transition, not dissolution, is a rare consolation left by such personalities to relatives and friends bereaved. It is independent of all creeds and philosophies: a conviction to be fostered if we are wise, if only because it is productive of a saner and truer habit of mind in thinking of our friend. That for the term of this life we have lost him, that in the height of his youth and promise his career has been cut short, is hard enough. But it is treason to the memory of one who had in his whole nature nothing akin to death to think of him as annihilated ; a condition, moreover, the possibility of which is an assumption as arbitrary and as repugnant to the developed consciousness as the crudest myth of primitive society. There is deep truth and justice underlying the saying of the dear old Abbé Jérôme Coignard : " Votre crapaud à tête de chat n'est pas plus véritable que la Nymphe de monsieur que voici ; *et de plus, c'est une invention dégoûtante.*"

Of such a quality of vital power and being was Philip Sidney Fletcher Nairn. And I have said so much to explain why in writing of my friend I will not use the tone of a funeral oration. According to medical authority, death came to him suddenly and painlessly on that May evening on the coast of Negri Sembilan. Changing his clothes for dinner after a motor drive, he was seized by an attack of hæmorrhage, and in half a minute all was over. He was spared the misery of an illness. It would have been difficult for those who loved him to wish him a more merciful ending. Nor is there any gain in dwelling on this last momentary sad scene of a full and happy life. To name him calls up his image in settings far different : his fine athletic figure at work in the " scrum," or braced against the wind on the Pikes of Scafell, or dark against the sunset on the level summit of the Pillar ; or deep in a big armchair reading aloud perhaps, Webster, Meredith, or Omar, talking of books or plays, spinning yarns, guessing at the riddles of the Sphinx, in some of our rooms at Trinity on one of those *noctes ambrosianæ*, sacred to youth and friendship, redolent of tobacco-smoke and

2

wine ; or on some wilder *nox Neroniana,* when the
bonfire shamed the stars, and as night grew old the
" Alpine Club," of which he was no obscure member,
went secretly forth to new conquests. Or, most familiar
to those who were with him in the East, the picture of
him that belongs to the last seven years of his life, living
the free active life that he loved, laying in able, thorough,
and human administration the foundations of a career
that promised to be of high distinction and Imperial
value.

In person, Nairn was what the sagas call *mikill ok
sterkr*—a big man and a strong. In height he was
over 6 ft. 3 in., and 13 stone in weight. Unlike many
tall men, he was well knit and well proportioned. His
complexion was very fair, until the tropics tanned it ;
his hair very fair, his features well cut, his eyes blue.
He was short-sighted and always wore pince-nez. His
voice was pleasant, strong, and expressive ; his laugh
big and merry, and of a quality to make others laugh
with him. At rest, his expression was grave and alert,
but the humorous lines were always ready to show themselves at the corners of his mouth and eyes. His manner
to strangers had a certain courtliness, but he could at
need be truculent enough. He was quick-tempered,
but not a bearer of malice. He was a good observer
and a judge of men. It was well said of him that his
friends prized his friendship the more because he did not
suffer fools gladly. The whole effect of his presence
was singularly buoyant and sunny. With his intimate
friends he adopted, when in good spirits, a tone half
mocking, half hectoring, and entirely delightful. The
nearest thing to it I can think of in literature is the
jesting bravado of Mercutio. Its charm is incom-
municable, except in so far as it may be caught in certain

passages of his diary and private letters reproduced in this volume.

Such letters and such extracts I make no apology for having introduced freely and fully, and with the least possible mutilation. A heavy responsibility must always attach to the giving of private letters to the general public. The justification for so doing lies in their value from a literary and biographical point of view. That expurgation, in the case of a document of real merit, means emasculation, is an axiom which Nairn always joined me in upholding; and I am concerned rather to present a true and lovable portrait of him to those who can appreciate it, than to perpetuate a washed-out travesty which shall appeal to the susceptibilities of persons whose opinion is negligible. Most of all I would not dim the impression of a spirit, which, had it encountered like misfortune, would have lived up to the example of that McPherson sung by Burns:

> Sae rantingly, sae wantonly,
>   Sae dauntingly gaed he;
> He played a spring and danced it round
>   Below the gallows tree.

CHAPTER II

FAMILY, BIRTH, AND SCHOOL LIFE

MR. HENRY NAIRN, who has taken some pains to investigate the early history of the Scottish house to which he belongs, has been led to the conclusion that all of the name of Nairn or Nairne are probably of common descent, going back to one Michael de Nairne, who lived at the end of the fourteenth century. This Michael signed as a witness, in his capacity of Shieldbearer to the Regent Albany, the compact of battle between the rival Clan Quhele and Clan Chattan before their fight described by Scott in his *Fair Maid of Perth*. The line has been carried back yet further, though with less certainty, to one Murdochus Nairne whose son, Hercules, witnessed a charter in 1211. It is matter for speculation whether the origin of the family was Keltic or Italian. Whatever may be the truth as to this, it is certain that the family is ancient, began with considerable dignity, and flourished for some centuries. Later it fell on evil days, and most of the estates passed into the female line.

The branch which concerns us made its home in Northumberland. William Nairn, the son of William Nairn who was Baillie of Dalkeith, appears to have left Scotland and settled in the parish of Kirkwhelpington, a remote village in the Cheviots near the Scottish border,

in or before 1737. In the following generations the
family moved to Rothbury and thence to Newcastle-on-
Tyne, where, about the year 1800, was established the
commercial firm well known in the North for over half
a century as Philip Nairn & Sons, shipowners and
corn importers. Philip Nairn of Waren, the son of
the founder of this firm, was a man of distinguished
personality, well known, popular, and respected by all
classes of people with whom he came into contact in
Northumberland, where for many years he enjoyed the
distinction of being the largest farmer and the largest
grain merchant between the Forth and the Tyne. In
politics a Whig of the old school, he was a powerful
supporter of Lord Grey when Prime Minister, of his son
Lord Howick, and of Sir George Grey of Falloden. This
political connection created an intimacy with the many
sons of the Prime Minister, all of whom were frequent
guests at the Waren dinner parties, which Mr. Nairn's
lavish hospitality and the charm, intellectuality, and
social gifts of his wife made famous throughout the
county. Nor were the guests at these dinners limited
to his own political party. He practically kept open
house; nobody, whatever his rank or position, left
Waren without partaking of its well-known hospitality,
and the servants' hall was rarely empty. In the early
fifties a series of disastrous losses of uninsured property,
combined with the effect of the introduction of telegraphy
which militated against the somewhat old-world methods
of Philip Nairn & Sons, and nullified the advantage
hitherto enjoyed by Mr. Nairn as indisputably one of
the best judges of corn in England, brought an end
to this prosperity. He moved to Wetheral, near
Carlisle, where he died somewhat suddenly in 1859.
His son, Mr. Henry Nairn, moved to London to take up

the clerkship in the Government Service which he held for over forty-two years.

One point, perhaps the most interesting of all, must be mentioned before I pass to the main subject. The descent of the Nairns of Northumberland from William Nairn, Baillie of Dalkeith, though it rests on the strongest circumstantial evidence, probably could not be proved in a court of law. If, however, as seems reasonable, this descent is taken as established, it connects the family by direct succession in the female line with William Drummond of Hawthornden, the poet and friend of Ben Jonson, and one of the most brilliant men of letters of the late Elizabethan times. If this be so, the poetical gifts which produced the verses which form this volume may reasonably be attributed to heredity throwing back in the ninth generation to Drummond of Hawthornden.[1]

[1] The descent from Drummond of Hawthornden is based on the following evidence :—

(a) The Nairns of Northumberland trace their descent direct from William Nairn who settled at Kirkwhelpington about the year 1737. This William came from Dalkeith in Scotland, and was the son of William Nairn, Baillie of that town.

(b) William Nairn, Baillie of Dalkeith, married on July 13th, 1701, Margaret Drummond, daughter of Sir John Drummond of Hawthornden, and granddaughter of the poet. The marriage is proved by the Baillie's will, of which the trustees were William Nairne of Dunsinane, Sir Alexander Cookham of Langton, William Drummond of Hawthornden, Robert Hume of Smeaton, James Nairn, and John Nairn "my brother."

The connexion thus depends on two assumptions :—

(i) That the William Nairn, Baillie of Dalkeith, mentioned in (a) above is identical with the William Nairn, Baillie of Dalkeith, mentioned in (b).

(ii) Further, that William Nairn of Kirkwhelpington was the son of the Baillie by Margaret Drummond, and not the son of any earlier or later marriage.

As to (i), the dates available support the identity, and it is unlikely

7

POEMS, LETTERS, AND MEMORIES

Philip Sidney Fletcher Nairn was born at Bromley, Kent, on December 11th, 1883 : the only son and youngest child of Mr. Henry Nairn, late of H.M. Civil Service. His mother died when he was only seven years old. She was a woman of singular charm, beloved by all who came into contact with her. From her her son inherited the charming personality which made him so popular with all who knew him, and also his linguistic talent; for, born in Naples and educated in Germany, she spoke with equal facility English, French, German, and Italian. Through her he descended from a branch of the Campbell family. His great-grandfather, an officer in a Highland regiment, on retiring from the Service settled at Naples, and married a Sicilian lady. Much of the Sicilian blood showed itself in Nairn in his childhood ; from the earliest age he gave signs of those dramatic, poetic, and imitative powers which there is little doubt descended to him from that histrionic race. His home was at Wimbledon from the time of his mother's death until he left England sixteen years later for the East.

At the age of seven he went to a dame's preparatory school at Wetheral, and two years later to Rokeby School, The Downs, Wimbledon, an excellent preparatory school managed by Mr. C. D. Olive, M.A., of Christchurch, Oxford. In 1896 he obtained a Founda-

that there should have been at the same or nearly the same time two persons named William Nairn both of whom were Baillies of Dalkeith. As to (ii), there appears to be no record of any other marriage.

The evidence is therefore very strong, if not conclusive. If accepted, it connects the Nairns of Northumberland by direct descent with William Drummond of Hawthornden. It connects them also, indirectly and remotely, with a long line of sovereigns of Scotland, Great Britain, and the United Kingdom, through one John Drummond of Carnock, whose son was an ancestor of the poet, and whose daughter Annabella became Queen of Scotland in the fourteenth century.

[*From a photograph by Lavender, of Bromley, Kent.*

FIVE YEARS OLD.

tion and a House Scholarship at the King's School, Canterbury. This is the oldest school in the British Empire, founded in the sixth century in the time of St. Augustine, and ideally situated in the precincts of Canterbury Cathedral.[1]

The Dean of Canterbury when Nairn was at school there was the well-known writer, Dr. Farrar. As an old Headmaster the Dean took a great interest in the King's School, of which, in his capacity of head of the Cathedral Chapter, he was principal Governor, and it was his custom always to have one of the sixth form boys to act as his unofficial and part-time private secretary and assist him in his correspondence. On Nairn's entering the sixth form he was selected by the Dean for this post. The Dean took a great personal interest in him, and often asked him to meet his distinguished guests at the Sunday morning breakfasts which were a feature of the Deanery hospitality. It was good for him intellectually, as well as entertaining, to listen to the conversation between his host and the celebrated divines, politicians, writers, and statesmen who were present on these occasions.

Nairn was very happy at Canterbury, where, as else-

[1] The school was founded by Theodore of Tarsus, second Bishop of Canterbury. It was renowned in the time of the Venerable Bede for its successful inculcation into its pupils of the Greek and Latin language and literature. After being carried on by the Benedictine monks without a day's intermission up to the period of the Reformation, it was refounded by Henry VIII in 1541 under the new title of the King's School. Among its famous scholars were the Lord Chancellor Thurlow; the Lord Chief Justice Tenterden; many Archbishops and Bishops; Harvey, the discoverer of the circulation of the blood; Boyle, the great Earl of Cork; and many other celebrated men. Last, but not least, "kind Kit Marlowe," the splendour of whose genius rivals that of Webster, and is surpassed only by Shakespeare's, in that constellation of poetic and dramatic achievement which is named the Elizabethan period.

where, he was successful in his studies and in his games. He rose to be Head Monitor, and was also Captain of the Rugby Fifteen and Champion Swimmer and Diver. Cricket he never excelled in, because of his defective eyesight. He was Vice-Captain of the school, and just missed becoming Captain.

His summer holidays were generally spent abroad—principally in Normandy—with his father and sisters, and were thoroughly enjoyed. In this way he came to know most of the north of France, besides parts of Belgium and Germany. His visits to Lindenfels and Eppstein in Germany covered the Odenwald and Bergstrasse, Frankfurt, and the Rhine from Rotterdam to Mayence; from Éprave and Hastière he journeyed over all the Forest of Ardennes, and visited Dinant, Brussels, and Bruges; while his holidays in Normandy at Arromanches, Langrune, St. Pierre, and at St. Jacut and elsewhere in Brittany, made him acquainted with nearly the whole country, including the " Suisse Normande."

CHAPTER III

OXFORD AND STETTIN

NAIRN came up to Trinity College, Oxford, in October 1902, and by virtue of being a Scholar (he had won two Exhibitions at Trinity, the Ford and the Rose) was given rooms in College at once, an advantage which is denied to many freshmen. He first had rooms on the Bell staircase in the Chapel Quad, and later in Kettle Hall, where he was a near neighbour to certain of the elect of the year immediately senior to his own, who had, according to compact, made their quarters in the New Buildings in close proximity, and among whom he was to form some of the most valued friendships of his Oxford days.

'Varsity life is a peculiar and precious growth of English soil—it were truer to say of Oxford and Cambridge soil. It is easy to miss getting from it the full measure of what it has to give, and these golden four years between boyhood and manhood may be wasted not less by undue application to study than by over-addiction to those distractions which abound by day and by night in and about our universities. Happy the man who can so spend those halcyon days as to feel, looking back in later years, regret indeed that they are past, but no remorse for lost opportunities, whether grave or gay, of storing his youth with experiences,

11

associations, discoveries, enthusiasms, friendships, that bear with them into the soberer years of after-life a flavour and a fragrance not elsewhere to be gathered. Nairn had, as not many men have, I think, this happiness, this power of high-spirited enjoyment of every side of life, guarded by the saving principle of μηδὲν ἄγαν.

After all, the purpose of Oxford is education : to it belongs the last step in that process before the tables are set for the serious game of life, where no false move can be recalled. And lectures and texts form but a small, and not perhaps the most important, part of the fountain of learning which an Oxford life affords. To the official side of the curriculum Nairn paid so much attention as to obtain a Third Class in Honour Mods. and a Second in History—a degree which would be in itself a credit to a man of moderate parts. To this it may be added that he played Rugby football for his college, and on one occasion played for the 'Varsity, though he did not obtain his blue. But the main part of his life at Trinity, and that to which I know he looked back with pleasure and affection, was represented by those social and intellectual activities which lie outside the rut of what is, after all, schoolboy work and play. I include under this head river excursions, motor drives, walks in the parks or the surrounding country, midnight symposiums, philosophic and unphilosophic, *andante piacevole* and *presto con fuoco*, wherein he took part not perhaps always wisely yet seldom too well ; activities, let me add (if any over-serious reader haply of the fairer sex should scent herein matter of offence), entailing no incident of which he or any sensible person need feel ashamed. *Dulce est desipere in loco.* It is to be set down to his wisdom and the soundness of his character in these merry opening years of manhood that these adventurous or Anacreontic interludes never reached the point of embroiling him seriously with the College authorities and imperilling his continued residence at that seat of learning. So far as I remember, the gravest charge he was called upon to answer was when he and certain jolly companions were haled before the Proctors and fined £2 apiece for paying their respects at a late hour to some attractive young ladies, not unconnected with the musical comedy stage, who happened to be staying a few days in Paradise Square.

Trinity at this time was in danger of becoming a somewhat " cliquey " college. It had, three or four years earlier, been rescued from a threatened anarchy of rowdyism by its new Dean, Mr. Michael Furse, now Bishop of Pretoria ; and a tendency had become apparent among a certain section of the undergraduates to look upon themselves as the peculiar guardians of the corporate welfare. Among the freshmen of the year 1901 there grew up a group of friends, including many of the scholars and one or two of the best rowing men and football players of the year, between whom and the just persons of the senior years there arose a degree of estrangement based, no doubt, on mutual misunderstanding. This lack of good fellowship was doubtless very silly, very unjust, very unnecessary on both sides, as plenty out of each camp have since discovered. It was pronounced, however, when Nairn came up in 1902.

It was in 1901, and among what I may call the Cæsarean as opposed to the Pompeian party, that the exclusive and august body known as the A.C. was founded. There were, I think, five original members, and the membership never went far beyond this. The initials stood for " Alpine Club," the object of the society being primarily climbing in and out of Trinity and other colleges in the small hours. To the jaundiced eye, however, of second-year virtue the letters signified " Alcoholic Club." That the principles of the body were *anti*-alcoholic I am certainly not so hardy as to allege. Its memory is enshrined in the famous Mitre Cup, the existence of which is due to Mr. Raper : a name that few Trinity men—not I, at least—can pronounce without a feeling of the warmest admiration and affection. The cup commemorates the unexplained appearance one morning in the Garden Quad at Trinity of a stone mitre, an architectural feature of St. John's College, and its equally unexplained disappearance and return to its age-long abode during the following night. Nairn was elected to the A.C. soon after becoming a member of the college, and took no mean share in some of its most successful enterprises. I think he was there when the President missed his hold in the dark on a certain fall-pipe high aloft on the " overland route," and had to be extricated from Balliol with a sprained ankle by means of sheets let down from a first-floor window looking on to Trinity quad. Other incidents are mentioned in his letters. In 1904 he writes :—

" The Alpine Dinner was a vast success, and also the flash-light photo thereof, but —— and ——, with their accustomed celerity, have not yet sent it me. To solemnise the occasion we lit an enormous bonfire in the middle of the Parks, which created intense scandalismos, and an unfortunate rencontre with a copper, suspicious of our numbers and presence at 4 a.m."

In 1906 he writes :—

" I suppose you saw all about *l'affaire Maurice*. It

may interest you to hear that I wasn't in it (though
I damned nearly was). Most of Trinity and no small
part of the 'Varsity still think I was, however. So
that spurious notoriety is descending upon me in my
reprobate old age." [1]

[1] The *affaire* in question, leading to the arrest of the gifted President
of the A.C., who, though he had gone down and taken his degree, was
apparently entered by the god on the occasion of a visit to his old
haunts and inspired to violate the sanctity of the roofs of New College,
formed matter for cold and uninstructed mention in the public prints.
I quote the following extracts, preserved in Nairn's book of press
cuttings :—

" The Vice-Chancellor's Court at Oxford was crowded with undergraduates yesterday, when Maurice Henry Woods, B.A., of Trinity
College, described on the charge-sheet as of no occupation, was charged
with being found on enclosed premises—viz. on the roof of New College
—supposed for an unlawful purpose, at 2.25 a.m. on Monday.

" A telephone message came to the police from the porter's lodge at
New College that three men were on the roof. The building was at
once surrounded, and after a time Woods was discovered and secured.
He had made a perilous descent of 30 ft. from the roof of the Warden's
house to the roof of the cloisters by means of a telephone wire.

" He was detained in the lodge while a search was made for the other
two men, but they escaped.

" The Warden of New College said that his daughters were alarmed
greatly by hearing the men on the roof. This was not the first time
men had climbed about his roof at night, and the inmates of his house
were terrified.

" The Vice-Chancellor was anxious to know why Woods was on the
roof at all, but the only explanation he received was that it was to
indulge in the amusement of climbing. Woods apologised to the
Warden for any inconvenience caused by his foolish act.

" The Vice-Chancellor decided that there was no proof of any unlawful purpose, and Woods would be discharged. But the discredit
and degradation he had brought upon himself by what could only be
called ' monkey tricks ' would be a severe punishment. The proctors,
moreover, would be able to deal with him in an effective manner."

It is sad to read, in the Vice-Chancellor's comments, the callous
judgment of a bourgeois world on the eccentric pastimes of a man of
brilliant attainments. Still, as Dogberry says, " God is to be worshipped : all men are not alike."

Whether the Club survived into later years or ended its existence with the going down of those who constituted it in its prime, history relates not, nor is it relevant to this narrative.

Though his particular friends were identified with what has been referred to as the Cæsarean camp, Nairn was *persona grata* with all sections of the College. His membership of the Rugby fifteen and of several of the college literary and debating societies, such as the *Griffin* (the official debating society of Trinity) and the *Gondoliers* (founded originally for the study of Gilbertian opera, but extending its patronage to a much wider range of dramatic literature), kept him in touch with the more orthodox elements. But the chief reason lay in his sunny and sociable disposition, the power of which no one who came into contact with him could long resist. Even the inner camp of irreconcilables unbent towards Nairn. In later years chance brought him into close relationship and good fellowship with some of those from whom college cliquishness had divided him at Oxford.

If the fascination of pleasant memories has trapped me into dwelling on the more " unbuttoned " side of the Oxford days, it must not be thought that he neglected their quieter gifts. He was a great reader, and no term or vacation passed without adding a number— sometimes a dozen, sometimes a score—of entries to the list he kept of books read : a long and catholic list, dating back to his preparatory school-days when he was only ten years of age. The short stories of Guy de Maupassant, Swinburne's *Poems and Ballads*, Meredith's *Shaving of Shagpat*, and various plays of Shakespeare and other Elizabethan dramatists were among his favourite books first read during his 'varsity days.

Many of these we discovered jointly, and read aloud together : some at Trinity on lazy afternoons, others at Mrs. Honey's among the Borrowdale mountains. He possessed the accomplishment, very rare because never taught, of reading aloud well, without monotony or affectation ; and it was equally delightful to listen to his rendering of the musical cadences of lyric poetry, or to his declamation, in a swashbucklering style that was peculiarly his own, of the thunder-charged dialogue of *Edward II* or *The Duchess of Malfi.*

His literary tastes and accomplishments are matter for a later chapter. The name of Borrowdale brings me to two vacations spent at the Lakes, in the springs of 1905 and 1906. Our headquarters were at Green Bank, a house standing back on the hillside behind the farm of High Lodore, half a mile or so from the head of Derwentwater and the same distance from the little hamlet of Grange and the Gates of Borrowdale. Here, fortified by the hospitality and good cheer of Mrs. Honey, we put in four hours' reading at our text-books each morning, supplemented by a less defined period in the evenings, and spent the rest of the day in exploring the high fells between Skiddaw and Scafell. The charm of the Lake mountains cast its spell on Nairn. He writes in 1909 from Kota Bharu :—

" I've been thinking of you in the tail-end of this year, up at Mrs. Honey's, when the vile tourists have left only their traces behind on the fells and visitors' books, and one can roam unoffended in the solitudes. *Jucundum fuerit !* Even in a glorious country like this, with the mountains all round, and the distant forests blue on the hillsides, or sailing on the sea in an open boat by night, with the stars reflected in the waters, and a cool breeze swelling the big sail—no, there is no moment like that on the high fells when the mists swirl and lift, and the dales appear in the sunlight below."

One expedition stands out clearly in my recollection. After our morning's work we set out, with the traditional change of stockings and a toothbrush, to climb Gable and the Pillar, descending to Wastdale Head, where we were to spend the night, and return by way of Eskdale next day. It was late spring and snow lay on the high mountains ; the wind had blown the ice on a post planted in the cairn on Gable into feathers some inches long. Breasting the ridge of Greyknotts we encountered a hail-storm that whipped our right cheeks to the hue of the rowan berry, and as the storm passed the clouds divided and revealed the Pillar, dark and wild against a white mist, the teeth and edges of his black crags picked out with snow, the sky leaden above him, and a rainbow thrown across cloud and hill. It was then, I think, that Nairn fell in love with the Pillar, which he considered the finest of the Lake mountains. We stood on the top of it at sunset, looking down to the vast bulk of the Pillar Stone and the shadowy depths of Ennerdale far below it, and westward to Ennerdale Water coloured with the sunset. It was dark by the time we had descended the abrupt grassy sweeps of the Black Sail, and we stumbled among many walls and stony water-courses before we reached the inn at Wastdale Head, where, since we had beards and no luggage and were plainly dirty, we felt ourselves something less than honoured guests.

Next day, after visiting the foot of Wastwater, we crossed by Burnmoor Tarn to Eskdale, and after a

18

At the Foot of Wastwater, April 1906.

18]

substantial tea at the Woolpack Inn started up the dale at 4.45. After passing Esk Falls, where two streams join and above which is a steep ascent into the wilds of Upper Eskdale, we found ourselves driven more and more to the left, being unable to cross the beck, which was greatly swollen by rain. Foreseeing the approaching alternative of an ignominious return to the Woolpack or a night spent on the inhospitable flanks of Scafell, we finally leapt, not without risk, the steep and rocky watercourse and gained the higher levels of the valley, desolate and grand beneath the savage buttresses of Scafell and the Pikes. But the way was longer than we had reckoned ; much time had been wasted in seeking a crossing-place ; and we had to run a race with the daylight to ensure our finding the track on Esk Hause before dark. We sped like chamois (but scarcely with chamois' speed or sureness of foot) along the huge and insecure boulders that cover the Eskdale slope of Esk Pike, halting at whiles to imbibe new energy from the brandy-flask, and reached Esk Hause as the deep crimson of the sunset was dying in the gap between Gable and the precipices of Great End, while Venus hung like a splendid jewel above it. The descent of Sty Head by starlight was slow. Once on the level we swung down the well-known road at five miles an hour. It was ten o'clock when we reached Mrs. Honey's. She had prepared roast duck, most succulent, for our supper. We ate it—I had almost said, the head with the legs and the appurtenances thereof. We slept a profound and dreamless sleep. Such feats can the digestion do in Borrowdale.

One day at Seathwaite, the little cluster of houses that lies highest in the main arm of Borrowdale on the way to Sty Head, we were late coming down from Bowfell: too late, in Nairn's opinion, for tea. He was for pressing on to Rosthwaite and beer; I, mindful of the excellence of the tea at Seathwaite, was for tea first and beer afterwards. The tea was ordered, but Nairn refused to share it, sitting over against me while I ate and drank, and heaping opprobrium upon me in picturesque and lurid terms, much to the consternation of the farmer's daughter. For drinking tea out of the saucer I was likened, with imprecations, to an old woman in a third-class railway refreshment-room. After tea we walked some few hundred paces in a thunderous silence (he told me afterwards that it was with difficulty that he refrained from striking me); then, at the same moment, we both burst out laughing, and there was peace again. Such and of such importance was this our most serious quarrel.

Other vacations he spent at home, or visiting friends, or travelling on the continent. In the Long Vacation of 1904, after staying up at Oxford for " Commem.," the Alpine dinner, and Trinity ball, he spent six or seven weeks coaching a man for Smalls, and most of the rest of the time at Wimbledon, where he reported himself as " slaving away at History, but it is devilish hard working at home, with various attractions." He stayed with a friend at Seaview in the Isle of Wight for Cowes Week that summer. " As my friend has a small yacht," he wrote before going, " and is a bit of a mariner, as well as an old rowing blue (Oxon), I am rather fancying myself doing a slight Lipton touch." The following letter shows what he was doing in the Long of 1905 :—

" LINDISFARNE, ELM GROVE, WIMBLEDON,
" *August* 3rd, 1905.

" O MOST EXCELLENT ONE,

" How much more excellent thou art than the

unworthy writer of these lines, lo ! thy two admirable but unanswered letters attest.

" I really feel that I owe you some apology for not writing—especially after your excessive research in the matter of Swiss hotels. My Guvnor was thinking of going over there, but has changed his mind and is going to Brittany. However, I expect the information will be of use another year.

" How went the viva ? I am anxious to see the lists. I suppose you saw —— staggered creation by taking a 3rd in law ?

"All my cubbing hopes and prospects have been cruelly dashed—it's a way these things have. My French Marquis was already bagged, and a billet in Cumberland at —— Hall, that seemed a snip, fizzled out at the last moment, as Lady —— was too ' broke' to afford such a luxury as myself. This was the real reason, the pretext being that her cubs were paying visits to friends.

" Another billet in Somerset also ' ran amok,' so I got bored and decided to go to Germany, and master (or at any rate acquaint myself superficially with) its uncouth Teutonic tongue.

" By the bye, on the strength of my Gallic scion of the nobility it was reported in Wimbledon that I was going out to India as tutor with a young English Duke— ' Sic fama volat et crescit eundo.'

" I am starting for Germany—Frankfurt a/M.—on Monday via the Hook, and expect to stay there about seven weeks. I am going to friends—a very jolly old house—about three miles out, and as there will be a lot doing in Frankfurt (including myself) I ought to make things lively. My greatest pang is that, when last I went to Germany, I never set eyes on a girl whom I did not do my best to forget at once. Still, the gods may be kinder now.

" By the bye, ' She ' is coming to stay in Oxford again in October—you will doubtless gather to whom I am referring, if you found me as unbearable about Eights Week as Ridley and other cold-blooded prosaics appear to have done.

" However, enough of myself, e'er you are quite nauseated by my egotism. What are you going to do ? How about the fair one in Paris ?

" By the bye, if you have not yet read *Diana*, do so at once—it is very fine. I am going to take several Meredith with me to read in Germany.

" I have been working (more or less) for the past month, and playing tennis nearly every day, but am getting very bored with England and anxious to get away. I saw Jim Gilkison the other day. His people have taken a shooting up in Forfar, and he wants me to go up and shoot the wily grouse (or at any rate pose as your murderous sportsman), but I had to refuse as I shall not be back.

" My address in Frankfurt will be :

c/o Herr Bartmann-Lüdicke,

Riederhöfe,

Frankfurt a/M.,

in case you feel magnanimous enough to answer this letter.

" Ever thine, " PHILIP NAIRN."

The lady of Eights Week was more than a transient attraction. It were unprofitable, besides impertinent, to speculate on what might have been. She inspired the most perfect of his poems.

Three weeks later he writes from Frankfurt :—

" August 24th, 1905.

" As you have, in a spirit of just retaliation, not deigned to answer the letter of your grovelling friend, I do myself the pain of writing to you yet again.

" I am fairly well satisfied with Germany, there are many worse places. I got fairly well fed up by my journey here. I had eleven hours in the train feeling like a bottle of medicine, ' to be well shaken while being taken.' This is a very jolly old house of twelfth century, with a ripping garden, about two miles out of Frankfurt. The Palmengarten here and the Opera are bully—I saw Verdi's *Aida* the other night, well sung and staged. I should go every night if the Germans did not habitually turn in by 10 p.m., and we are out about three miles from the Operahaus. I was over at Homburg the other day, in the Taunus Mountains, no end of a flick place. Beauty is rare. However, I met a rather jolly girl yesterday, who is staying an hour's walk from here across the country, and I find I can always learn a foreign tongue better from a pretty girl. Ireland is, however, in no danger. I am making vast progress in German, and shall be quite sorry to leave here, which I do in about a month. Where are you ?

" Ever yours,

" P. S. N."

The next two letters belong to the beginning of his fourth year, when most of his friends of the year senior to his own had gone down :—

> "21, MICHAEL ST.
> "*Friday, October 20th,* 1905.

"MY DEAR OLD MAN,

"What the blazes can have happened to you ? Where are you and what are you doing ? Moreover, when are you taking your degree and why have you not written to me ? Are you at Wren's or are you in love ?

"These are just a few of the questions I should like answered.

"Here I am in Oxford once more, where the cold is damnable, and the place deserted by most of those tried old friends whose footsteps resounded erstwhile on the paving of Cornmarket Street.

"Pot and MacB. were here a day or two ago, previous to a three-months sojourn in Hanover—to-morrow I believe they are contemplating giving a 21ster (pray note the gibe) to the marine denizens of the North Sea.

"Milly is reported due here to-night at 8.10.

"Sid Field is reported assiduously polishing a high stool in a Leamington office. Duggy Graham is once more here (at Marcon's Hall) and Maurice ably adorns the Presidential Chair.

"The G—— is married and H—— (my God !)—I still detest.

> "Ever yours,
> "PHILIP S. NAIRN."

24

OF PHILIP SIDNEY NAIRN

" OXFORD UNION SOCIETY,
" *November 5th,* 1905.

" MY DEAR HERRICK,

" I am rejoiced to hear that we meet again at Philippi on the 9th inst. Can't you make it more than a flying visit ? Of course you understand that you will put up at the hotel—21, Michael St.—so many people drop in that we have had to christen the diggs. ' St. Michael's Hotel '—less charitable people may designate it—the pub.

" I suppose you are working very hard; so am I. One H—— don and I are at loggerheads, and from rather doubtful collections he is piling on the weekly tale of essays, in the idea that I am more ignorant than I should be—a year off schools. A sublime error on his part, except in the matter of constitutional history, which makes me inclined to spew up the little knowledge of it I possess.

" P. is chucking slice-eating : a good thing for him, as he was acquiring fresh vices in Chichester—a most banausic spot, in which the only society to be found was in the local bars. He and W—— are going in for the consular service. I am going to have a slap at the Egyptian Civil, but doubt whether I have any chance, as they will probably plough me over eyes.

" Do you know Ernest Dowson's poems ? John Long has just brought out a new *5s.* edition. I like his poems immensely.

" I went with Duggy Graham to hear Yvette Guilbert last night. She is magnificent—if you have a chance, don't fail to see her. I wish to heaven I could hear

25

her sing that portion of her repertoire which I fear did not pass the Vice-Chancellor's blue pencil.

"To-night I am going to the Ouds to hear one of the 'Follies' at a smoking concert. I am going as my Twin's guest. It is quite useful his being on the Ouds.

"Ever yours,

"P. S. N."

Nairn, like most of his friends, worked prodigiously hard in the months preceding his schools, but he also kept up a wonderfully good average of reading both in term time and in the vacation for a man of such varied interests and so sought by, and seeking, society. It had been Dean Farrar's wish that he should become a schoolmaster, a calling for which he considered him peculiarly fitted; and this was the career that Nairn had in mind when he came up to Oxford. In the event, however, his degree was not destined to prove a sufficiently brilliant one to give him the best start for an academic life. Moreover, he did not look forward to such a life with any lively pleasure. And so it was that some time before his History finals were in sight he was contemplating a preferable alternative in the Egyptian Civil Service, the posts in which were to be filled for the first time by a system of limited competition wherein mere " bookish theoric " was to count for less than the qualities of leadership and *savoir faire* which he possessed in so marked a degree.

"I am working like hell—eight hours a day," he writes early in 1906, " and also putting in for the Egyptian touch, but as there are about eighty applicants from either 'Varsity and about twelve berths, the chances of success are not rosy. I spent a very merry ten days with the Fields at Leamington. The rest of the vac. I did about four hours a day."

A little later he writes :

"UNION SOCIETY, OXFORD,
"*Sunday, March 11th,* 1906.
"DEAR RIC,

"Thanks frightfully for your frequent letters. I'm sorry I have not answered them before.

"I suppose you have fixed it up all right with Mrs. Honey? I am looking forward to it very much. I go down to Painswick (Glos.) on 17th, immediately after collections, to stop with Brucie for a few days, but I shall be home before 30th.

"How goes it with you? your letters tell me so little about yourself. H—— and I are almost amicable now, as I took a pure *a* on a collection of Stubbs's Charters. We have two more at end of term, one on my Foreign Period, which I know, and the other on my Special Period, which it will take all the cunning I possess to survive, without betraying the fact that my knowledge of it, if not elementary, is still very superficial.

"I have been rather North-Oxfording it this term : progressive bridge, whist, etc. Result—acquaintance with one really nice girl, but she, alas! has now departed for Portugal.

"Adieu,
"Yours ever,
"P. S. N.

"P.S.—My application for E.C.S. is now awaiting consideration. Pray for me."

Nairn did not obtain the Egyptian appointment. On coming down from Oxford, in order to occupy his time profitably and improve his knowledge of German, pending his entering on a definite career, he went, under an arrangement then in force between the British and the German Education Departments, as English master to the Schiller Gymnasium at Stettin in Prussia, where he was to learn German in exchange for English. Here he spent many pleasant months, and here as elsewhere he was popular with the professors and the students. The following extracts from his diary kept in 1907 give a picture of his life in Germany. They cover the last six weeks or so of his time there :—

" *January 3rd.*—Bundled out of the train [1] at 5.30 this morning feeling very sleepy. This wore off after a cup of coffee at the station. Drove to ' Hotel Stadt London,' deposited my bag, and then explored Berlin in the half-light. Night was like day. Berlin life is continually looping the loop ; it is like a cat chasing its own tail. Visited the market early. Very interesting. Then came back, shaved, dressed and washed. Saw the Schloss, Dom, statuary, and modern pictures before lunch, which I had ' Unter den Linden ' about 3. Later went to Café Opera : good music. Met a very decent German—travelled, and dressed in London—with whom I spoke for about two hours. Then went to Kleine Theatre, and saw Oscar Wilde's ' Idealer Gatte ' very fairly well played—150th time. Had supper 'Unter den Linden ' and then walked in Friedrich Strasse for some time. At about two turned in. Feeling tired.

[1] At Berlin.

" *January 4th.*—Made a thundering good breakfast, and then armed with a map sallied forth to see the sights. In evening went to Winter Gardens—a huge music-hall with a starred room which made one feel one was *à la belle étoile*. Met a very decent American here, a full head taller than myself, an opera-singer anxious to learn German, very travelled, and the last ten years in Italy. Afterwards we went to the Westminster Café, excellent music. Then I had supper at Scandinavia, and eventually turned in about 3 a.m. In true British fashion the American and I never exchanged names, though we were together for about three hours.

" *January 5th.*—Had my chocolate rather late. Then went to the Friedrich Museum, and saw the Dutch, Spanish, and Italian Masters, staying there till closing time at 3. A really grand collection. At about 4 I then lunched at the Luitpold Restaurant in the Friedrich Strasse.

" Left by the 7.30 train for Stettin, reaching there at 9.30. Frau —— like an owl had lighted no fire. It was cold and cheerless. I had some supper in my diggs., and not feeling very well went to bed soon.

" A city where one does not know a soul is no better than a desert, and I was glad to get away. It is so dreary to walk unendingly through a crowd of unknown faces.

" *January 6th (Sunday).*—After lunch I slept for the first time since I've been here, conforming to the general German custom. In the evening went to Sauft's where they jumped all over me.

" *January 9th.*—This morning I received a letter from Edith, enclosing one from the Editor of the *Pall Mall Magazine.* He has accepted my Sonnet ' In the Buchheide ' and offers me £1 1*s.* for it. Well, of course I just took it. Wrote a long ' board and lodging ' in German to Auntie G——. Supped at the ' Old Suftdichten ' in the Breite Strasse on bread and cheese—but the beer is A1. In the evening began Hauff's ' Lichtenstein,' having finished Zola's ' Kunstler-Leben.' I am now beginning a very strenuous and simple life, and having a real hard onslaught on the impregnable rock of German Grammar.

" *January 12th.*—Amicitia Wintergest and Dance. Am just back and it is 4.15 a.m. Quite good fun. Met a girl who really dances top-hole—a Fr. Paula ?—she taught me the ' open waltze,' which is really jolly. Old Stein, father of one of my pupils, fairly lifted the biscuit for friendliness, inviting me to stop with them in the country, and also standing me my dinner and wine. Really jolly old boy. Afterwards we went to the Kaiserkrone for a short time.

" *January 13th (Sunday).*—Went to the evening service at Jacobi Church. A very fine preacher—on Temperaments. To-day he treated the choleric temperament. He spoke excellent German, very clear and distinct. Shall go again.

" *January 15th.*—Just back from the Stadt Theatre, where I've seen Ibsen's *Pillars of Society*—really well done. I had only had time to read the first act beforehand. I think it is a pity that it does not end as a tragedy—the end seems to me to be an anticlimax—but I must first study the piece. . . . Frau —— gave me coffee, and jawed thereat for three hours.

" *January 16th.*—Met quite a pleasant musician from the Monopole at Saufts, where I was also induced to lose 60 pf. at dice.

" *January 19th.*—Had my ' abend brot ' at a real low-life tavern, which I shan't visit again in a hurry. Then came back and read the first two acts of Lessing's *Nathan der Weise* before I toddled to bed. They tell me it is a great play, but so far I can't see signs of it."

It was at this time that Nairn was invited to offer himself as a candidate for the post of Assistant to the British Resident at the Court of the Raja of Kelantan, in Siamese Malaya. He appears to have made up his mind at once to accept, though the natural anxiety of his family delayed the final decision for a week or two. That decision was momentous enough, for it affected the whole course and character of his later career. In terms the engagement was for three years, starting at £300 a year, with furnished house, and rising to £350 for the second, and £400 for the third year ; a re-engagement might follow by mutual consent. What swayed Nairn, however, in making his choice was, I think, the prospect of a free and absorbing life in new and intensely interesting surroundings, opening up a field of endless possibilities of travel and new experiences. He never regretted his choice.

Here is the entry in his diary recording the arrival of this fateful offer. The extracts which follow it bring to a close the time of his residence in Stettin.

" *January* 21*st*.—This morning I received a totally unexpected and astonishing letter from Raper, offering me the *chance* of a post in the Malay States, Assistant to British Resident of the Sultan of Kelantan, 150 miles north of Singapore; furnished house, £300 a year, and after three years six months' leave! I've applied, and shall now hear in three weeks, and if I get it, sail in seven. It is all so astonishing, and may lead to anything.

" However, I am not sanguine, though I broke glass yesterday, and again to-night, smashing a lamp in the kitchen in trying to find matches, and Frau —— says that's luck. She spent three hours this afternoon teaching me to write German letters. One thing is certain—whatever happens, stick hard to German and take life as if nothing had happened. I must confess it has given me a restless feeling.

" *January* 23*rd*.—20 grades of cold. This morning I invested in a pair of skates (5 mks.), and spent the whole morning in the eis-bahn in the Bismarck Platz. Very few people. The little kids (boy and girl) of the Consul Bernal came up and spoke to me quite naturally. The little girl was quite one of the most charming and self-possessed little mites I've ever seen. When she is older, she'll be a ripper.

" After lunch (at Saufts) there were a lot of people— and about twenty kids from the school, who followed me about everywhere. The Pied Piper of Hamelin was not nearly such a draw as I was in my old knicker-bocker suit.

"*January 24th.*—To-day I added to my acquaintanceship a little waiter who had once been in the 'Trocadero.' I know fishmongers, music players, tradesmen, tramps, etc.—a regular 'farrago vitæ.'

"*January 26th.*—In the afternoon we were pursued by the same host of small children. Really they have no manners, and their idle inquisitiveness is indecent. German schools ought to have corporal punishment.

"In the evening was the Zapfen Streich, or torchlight procession for the Kaiser's birthday, rather a jolly sight. But the massed bands were the attraction, and not loyalty. Nobody showed any enthusiasm for Willy, and a stranger would not have gathered that it was meant for an honour to the Emperor.

"*January 27th (Sunday).*—Saw the birthday parade in the Parade Platz—a good show, 7,500 troops, splendid marching, and the slope so perfect. A very large crowd present, but little real enthusiasm. In the afternoon went to tea at the Bernals'. They were quite charming to me, eventually pressing me to stay to supper, and finally Bernal and I discussed whisky and soda and colonial experiences till 2.30. I liked them very much, and everything about the flat was English comfort— the very antipodes of everything German. The Consul was first in Delagoa Bay and then in Rio Grande in Brazil. I think I really 'went down hellish well,' as George would have said, but it was rather a bit thick for an afternoon call. Forgot my house-key, but got in by dint of stirring up the baker.

"*January 31st.*—Finished friend Nathan—a dull

play, but the fable of the three rings in Act III is fine—
one could say the one good thing.

"*February 3rd (Sunday)*.—Supper at the Consul's,
which was charming. He does you very well in wine,
and in stories, but my old rule about leaving out port
if I'm going to take whisky is an axiom in connexion
with my idiosyncrasies.

"*February 6th*.—Read Schiller this morning. Post-
man brought me an official letter. The dingy dogs
want me to pay 'steuer.' I am going to protest.
Tried to translate a poem of Heine this afternoon, but
I've stuck.

"*February 7th*.—Bernal wanted me to dine with
him at Klettner's, but I had to refuse, as I'd fixed
up the *Meistersinger*. The piece lasted five hours,
and in parts the music made me quite sleepy, it
seemed to steal away and drown all my thinking
powers.

"*February 8th*.—Saw Frau —— who wanted to charge
me for the whole of March—but I'm damned if I'm
paying."

On February 11th he was on his way back to England, and on the 16th he learnt that he had been selected
from among a number of other candidates for the
Kelantan appointment. A month was spent in pre-
parations and farewell visits, and on March 16th he
left Charing Cross for Dover, lunching on the train
between Calais and Paris, at Paris dining solitary at
——'s "for auld lang syne, very sadly," and thence
taking the night express for Marseilles.

" All through the night," he writes, " slept fitfully. Then at eight watched the queer rocks and stunted olive trees and the grey Mediterranean, looking like a tame inland lake. Then Marseilles with all its southern sun and semi-eastern picturesqueness, redolent of Monte Cristo. After parting with a good many francs eventually got installed on the *Salazie*. Very few English passengers. We left about 12.30, and at nightfall were still coasting along within sight of the rocky southern coast."

CHAPTER IV

KELANTAN AND THE FEDERATED MALAY STATES

EIGHTEEN days after reaching his destination Nairn wrote a letter which far better than any second-hand account gives the incidents of his voyage and his first impressions of the East. It is as follows :—

> " KOTA BHARU, KELANTAN,
> " *May 4th*, 1907.

" DEAR OLD THING,

" Though I detest writing letters—it is the loathsome serpent that confronts me in this fair Eden— yet do I think that you deserve a letter, not as your right, but as a form of retribution—the only one that I can adopt towards you—which shall make your pallid cheeks grow red with shame.

" The old order of things has changed with a vengeance. England and all it means seems like a glimpse of Derwentwater caught for a moment through the wreathing mist on the top of Esk Hause—that day we tried Glaramara and failed. At times England comes back to your thoughts in a momentary vivid flash, at other times everything is a mere blur, 8,000 miles away, and in the never-failing interest of fresh scenes you live only for what is around you, and cast no backward regrets on the past. All is so new, and so beautiful; blue skies, and burning sun glowing in the pitiless dome of heaven, tropical vegetation, brilliant flowers, and graceful palms and young cocoanut trees looking like feathered arrows shot straight to earth by some Herculean Apollo from Olympus. And then at evening the brilliancy of the tropical night, the distant vivid flashes of summer lightning, like searchlights at play, the soughing of the wind in the creaking thickets of impenetrable bamboo, the bright moon flooding the river-stream with studs of silver light, the murmurous hum of insects, and the cry of strange animals in the jungle afar. It is impossible for me to give you all the new impressions that crowd upon me. One feels these things better than one can express. I sometimes could wish with the Psalmist that my pen was that of a ready writer. I think it was the Psalmist, but I'm open to rebuke.

" Well, of course I had a great voyage out. Like an Israelite I passed through the Red Sea, marvelled at the arid wastes of desert by the Canal, and worshipped the going down of the sun in Egypt as fervently as any Persian. Egypt of all lands is the land of sunset and sunrise. Nowhere do I think has night such charms. The very breath and look of the evening air hypnotises one, and is said to cause among the other sex insane acts of erotic origin. I'm told 'tis wise to look after women-folk well in Egypt. Sightseers at the palatial hotel at Assouan go off the rails as openly and more successfully than Potiphar's wife.

" My great pal on board was Captain Young, the
salvage expert, who saved the guns of the *Montague*
after they had been given up by the Admiralty. We
also had the Rector of Hatfield on board, Lord Will.
Cecil, and his spouse—Lady Florence. We had various
people, Egyptians, Hungarians, and Germans, but
nearly all the rest were French, and I had a great time.
I organised sports [1] and a fancy-dress dinner and ball,
going myself as a doll, with red wig, diaphanous chemise,
white socks and bare legs. Many people thought the
costume almost indecent ; but you know me better
than to suppose I would sully that fair robe in which
virtute me involvo.

" The sunsets in the Indian Ocean, the deep blue of
the sea like in *Off Valparaiso*, the clearness of the
atmosphere, beggar all description. After the rocky
wastes of Horeb, where poor old Moses tripped and
broke his stone tables, and the benighted Jews lost
their way for forty years, it was a heaven of beauty ;
on and ever on for a week, without sight of land, and
often ourselves and flying fish the only things of life
in all this wilderness of sea. And then Colombo, the
real taste of the East. Egypt is only the portal, the
mixture of East and West. Colombo : the first joys

---

[1] " To-day the sports, ' under the distinguished patronage of Mme.
V——,' came off, and were really a huge success. Three-leg races, egg
and spoon, shooting corks off bottles, filling in supplementary portions
of an ox—designed on the deck by me with great éclat—cock-fighting,
etc., were the order of the day. I won the three-legged ; prize-giving
in the evening by Mme. B——, followed by dancing. I got very nice
photo of *Salazie* as a prize. Altogether a great day."—*Extract from
diary, March 28th.*

of tropical vegetation and swift jinrickshas, the persistent hawkers of jewels and costly silks ; all the cunning, the picturesqueness, the avarice of the East ; Colombo, the Mecca of the world-traveller.

" At Singapore I had a week to wait, and was put up in lavish style by people to whom I had an introduction. And then on here in an odd little steamer for three more days.

" And now here I am at the end of my third week, already so accustomed to Eastern life that London and its grinding buses and shrieking newsboys seems an unpleasant dream, effected by a surfeit of lobster, cucumber, or what settled that hoary villain John, peaches and tinned salmon. Or is my history again at fault ? [1]

" Far from being the back of nowhere, this is civilisation. We have tennis every day, riding most days before breakfast. Climate is perpetual summer, and near to heaven. Mornings and evenings are delightfully cool; days as hot, but brighter far than Hades.

" Quickly am I learning to speak Malay. Officially I am Inspector of Police. We have a force of sixty Sikhs, military police for escorts and ornamental purposes. My civil police (Malays) at present are 200, but I expect to have 600 under me in a year or two. At present I learn Malay, and return salutes in the style of my volunteering salad days.

" When I command the Sikhs I am to have white

[1] Without access to the menu, I should not like to question it. My history book says that John, after grossly over-indulging himself one night at Newark Abbey, perished suddenly in October 1216.—E. R. E.

uniforms, stars, facings, sword, and glittering helmet. Yet do I scorn these trappings of office, though I hope I shan't look much of an ass. I have any amount of work before me, only wish you were here to share with me a bungalow, and talk of literature as in the old days. I shall never regret that I turned my attention from teaching little boys to brown-limbed cattle-lifters.

" Farewell,

" Yours ever,

" P. S. N.

" P.S.—Kindest regards to your people—and Old Coleridge.—P. S. N."

He spent five days in Singapore, staying with the Siamese Consul, Mr. Anderson, who treated him with the greatest hospitality. Here he made various purchases, and was introduced to the Chief of Police, who showed him all over the police system and gave him a good many hints about the work. On the 13th he sailed from Singapore in what he describes as a queer old boat slow as a snail, Danish built, whose decks were crowded with Malay and China natives, so that it was scarcely possible to move. Two Danish officers, a Norwegian first mate, two Chinese, an old Cumbrian planter, one M——, living twenty miles from Kota Bharu—

"A young planter from Selangor, one Y——, and a bounder to boot; this was our saloon," says his diary, " but still a very cheery crowd. Skipper had bought a fine large gramophone in Singapore, and we turned it on always after dinner. ' Teasing,' ' Departure of the Troopship,' ' Rosie, you are my posie,' etc., etc., mixed with the valse from *Faust* and one or two German songs—it was bought of a German-Jew firm. . . . Stopped at Trengganu, which for me was very interesting ; crowds of natives coming off in sampans. Read Hichens's *Woman with the Fan*, the psychology of which is damned good. T—— full of yarns of Kelantan, etc., etc. He's one of the oddest men I've met, with a bright red face, and apparently afflicted with prickly heat. He has also a funny little half-swallowed laugh, and he laughs at what no one else does, or else fails to hear, and wouldn't be funny if one did. Slept on bridge."

At the mouth of the Kelantan River he was met by the Resident's galley, manned by four men in khaki, and blue caps, who rowed him up. " They were merry fellows," he says, " and we got on well. After a time we sailed, and the remaining eight miles were for me Seaview over again, as I took the tiller and managed the sheet." And so, on April 16th, just a month after leaving England, Nairn came to Kota Bharu, where he was to remain under most enjoyable conditions for over two years, fortunate in his work, in his colleagues, and above all in his chief.

Kelantan is the largest of those Malay States which were at that time under the suzerainty of the King of Siam. A large part of the country lies in the basin of the river of the same name, a grand stream 120 miles long, and at Kota Bharu nearly a quarter of a mile broad. In the north-east, where it borders on the China Sea, the land is flat and fertile. Inland it rises to hilly country, culminating in mountain ranges which attain, on the confines of Pahang, Perak, and Rahman, a height of five, six, or even eight thousand feet. The land is rich in natural resources; the climate in the open and cultivated regions is mild and healthy, free from the more violent changes of temperature which belong to tropical countries, and in particular from the stifling heat at night. The population numbered at the census of 1912 about 287,000, the great majority of whom were Malays. The only town is Kota Bharu, on the east bank of the river. It has about 10,000 inhabitants, and is, thanks to Mr. Graham's sanitary reforms, one of the cleanest towns in the East. It is a garden city, with trees everywhere except in the main street and central market; " the streets appear to be woodland glades, and the houses peep out of a forest of palm, cocoanut, and rubber trees; the smooth broad sandy paths which represent the streets are pleasantly shaded by this abundant and grateful greenery."

Kelantan, like the neighbouring states of Kedah, Trengganu, and Perlis, was a very ancient dependency of Siam. The system of government, however, which was in force when Nairn arrived in April 1907, had existed for less than four years. In December 1902 an agreement had been entered into between H.M. the King of Siam and H.H. the Raja of Kelantan, providing for the appointment by the former of a Resident Commissioner to reside at the Raja's Court and act as his adviser. The internal administration of the State was henceforth not to be interfered with by the Siamese Government so long as the advice of the adviser was followed by the Raja in all matters other than those touching the Mahommedan religion. It was as first Resident Commissioner under this agreement that Mr. Walter Armstrong Graham came to Kelantan in July

1903. He found there a condition of administrative chaos. The Raja, unable single-handed to deal with the intrigues of his powerful kinsmen, retained only the outward semblance of power; the productive resources of the country were allowed to stagnate; the Courts of Justice were both corrupt and helplessly inefficient. The new Resident, however, a man of rare wisdom, tact, and knowledge of men, was equal to the situation. The existing conditions were due to no inherent faults of character in the people, and to no deficiencies of natural resources in the country, which was potentially a rich and prosperous one. By the exercise of great patience and skill he succeeded in winning over to the side of good government the very personages whose private interests had been served, to the detriment of the State, by the existing conditions. Consenting at first but grudgingly in the establishment of a reformed administration, they eventually entered with much goodwill into the duties of the high offices which they held under the new system. Once past the anxieties of the initial stages, the Resident was able to look forward with confidence to the successful and continuous development of the country under a settled and beneficial form of government.

The first month or two at Kota Bharu were spent by Nairn in learning the work, the people, and the language. The other three British officials serving under Mr. Graham—Mr. H. W. Thomson, Mr. H. E. Pennington, and Mr. C. A. H. Keenlyside—were all old Trinity men, and the two last had been up at Trinity with Nairn, two years his senior.[1] Keenlyside, like Nairn, had just come out to Kelantan, and for a time they shared a

[1] Both Pennington and Keenlyside have fallen in their country's service in the present war.

bungalow. The Residency stood just outside the town, on the river bank, surrounded by many acres of tropical garden kept by an army of Malay gardeners in perfect order. The three bungalows occupied by the four British members of the staff were scattered about the grounds within a few minutes' walk of the Residency itself, and the whole was surrounded by strong fencing. At the main entrance was stationed a Sikh guard, ten men strong, which was turned out to present arms whenever one of the Residency staff appeared.

The day after his arrival Nairn was formally introduced to the Raja, who " expressed surprise that I was not more than twenty-three, and said I looked clever. He evidently thinks me an expert." He was introduced on the same day to the Raja's uncle, the Tungku Sri Maharajah ; it was under this prince as his official superior that he was to hold the office of Superintendent of Police. Nairn doubtless felt himself far from an expert, so far as his prospective official duties were concerned. The police, who constituted the only armed force in the State, had, prior to 1903, been little better than a rabble, not so well disciplined and about as useful for practical purposes as the force presided over by Dogberry and Verges. Subsequently, after some attempts at reform had proved ineffective, drastic measures had been taken. These had met with a good deal of success, but plenty of room for improvement remained at the time of Nairn's arrival.

A picture of his life in Kelantan may be put together from the following extracts from his diary :—

" *April* 18*th*.—Up at 6, and found our two horses waiting at 6.30. Joined Mr. and Mrs. Graham at the corner. Of course I was rather nervous, but ' Weary

AT OXFORD, ON THE CHERWELL.

NAIRN'S BUNGALOW AT KOTA BHARU.

Willie' was patient with me, and I got on well enough not to fall off. First of all Graham and I inspected the Sikhs' drill, and it was really A1. Then we had a fine gallop. I shall be a bit sore to-morrow. Spent the whole morning learning Malay with a sergeant at the station. After tiffin discussed my duties with Graham. Went up to Club in the evening, and then watched the sunset and the bathers from the river's bank. It was marvellous—all crimson, flame-red, and orange.

"*April* 19*th*.—Friday—the Mahommedan Sunday, and our mail day. Slept after lunch. It is odd how post-prandial slumber dodges the Sabbath, wherever man chooses to keep it. Went up to Graham's and we had two good sets of tennis.

"*April* 21*st*.—A Canadian, a Mr. Crawford, had arrived, walking round the world without scrip or money in his purse, for some newspaper. Learnt Malay words all the morning. At tea went up to Graham's, where there is a weekly tea-fight with badminton for rajas.

"*April* 22*nd*.—To-day the Raja got up a bull-fight to show Crawford, the first of the season. It was quite a fierce affair : two bulls were led in to face each other. There was no furious charging ; they started scrapping with their horns, which were mostly interlocked. The fight continued till one was driven from the field amidst the cheers of an excited gathering. There was none of the Spanish business. Dined with Thomson, who introduced an Indian conjuror who is just leaving Kelantan —very good. Mr. and Mrs. Graham and Fergus came over to see.

" *April 23rd.*—Played tennis at the Grahams'. Crawford and Thomson dined with us, and he was quite good company. Our cook gave us a quite creditable dinner, and we had borrowed a good many things in the way of glass and plate from Thomson, so we made an opulent show.

" *April 24th.*—A great Mahommedan festival. Went for a walk along river-bank before breakfast. In evening watched a show at the mosque, of which I could not see much. Dined at Graham's, eight of us altogether. We all sat round and talked afterwards, which to my mind was infinitely superior to bridge.

" *April 25th.*—Lesson with Mahomed before breakfast. Went down to office. A traveller from Robinson's, Singapore, turned up and wanted to sell me things. Apparently my old Tungku had had thirty dollars' worth of cloth there, when he was in Singapore three years ago. He now repudiated it, and Mahomed was had in to interpret. The scene lasted an hour and was ludicrously Gilbertian; a prince and a traveller haggling over thirty dollars' worth of paltry cloth. Moreover, I am sure the old boy was lying, as he kept shifting his arguments, which were of the flimsiest.

" *April 26th.*—In the afternoon I fell asleep over the *Wrecker* at one of its most exciting scenes. So potent is the Sabbath in bringing the purple-lidded, poppy-laden sleep. Played tennis at the Grahams', but though starting well, eventually when playing with Pennington could do nothing. A Sikh came up to bring me an Indian paper—the Sikh organ—as a present.

" *April 27th.*—A blazing hot day. At office I picked up a small clerk with whom to talk, answering to name of Jemama.

" *April 28th.*—Had Mahomed before breakfast, and talked to my little clerk in the morning. Had half an hour's talk with the groom before lunch. Played tennis at the Grahams'. Everyone was there, including Crawford, who is really off to-morrow. He has been waiting all this time for an elephant.

" *April 29th.*—At office all morning, where I had an amusing interview with a polyglot Malay, who said he had been robbed, and was an employee of Duff. In the afternoon I took half a dozen photos of street life in Kota Bharu, and met Mahomed at the Post Office, when I talked for some time. Played tennis at the Grahams'. Dined at Thomson's. Quite nice. Played bridge afterwards.

" *May 2nd.*—Saw a great show at the mosque—Feast of Circumcision. It was more like pantomime with the properties of Aladdin. In the house of the old Raja, the scene was something like Christmas at the Riederhöfe. Played tennis at the Club a little. We all dined at Thomson's, including Fergus. Played bridge; I revoked, and that ended the chapter.

" *May 3rd.*—Took a long solitary up the river, and had the gratification of seeing a bonny blaze—three houses completely burnt up, like so much tinder. Even some of the trees close to the houses were also burnt.

" *May 5th.*—Ride with Mr. and Mrs. Graham before breakfast. Spent morning with Graham talking about my prospective duties, and afternoon with Jemama talking Malay at the office.

" *May 8th.*—Had my first lesson in reading Arabic characters. Spent whole morning at Police Station.

" *May 11th.*—Kit inspection of the barracks before breakfast. Graham has an eagle eye that sees everything, and I have plenty of work before me. Tungku was ill, and I was in command at the office, and had a lot of offenders to deal with. Stayed there without tiffin till 3 p.m.

" *May 13th.*—Inspected barracks and then the gaol. Long day at the office. Succeeded in sacking one of our ' alien ' policemen for his tenth offence. Row between Sikhs and warders. Have decided to give up tiffin and make a big tea with eggs at 3 p.m. Find it answers much better, and all the more important work comes at mid-day as the Tungku is always late.

" *May 14th.*—Played tennis at the Grahams'. We afterwards dined there, and played bridge, which I tried in vain to escape, and consequently enjoyed immensely. *La vie!*

" *May 16th.*—Attack on one of the judges, but at present no means of lagging the culprit. It seems impossible to get any pay—all through the influence of some damned treasury-clerk. Went up to the Club, where a football match took place between police and club, both sides cheering themselves on vigorously.

" *May 23rd.*—Went out riding with Pen. Very jolly morning, but my gee, swerving from a post, flung me head first into a ditch, and I thought I had broken my neck. At any rate I was damned sore, and for a time fairly dizzy.

" *May 24th.*—Had a rotten headache all day, possibly partly due to my antics yesterday morning, but also Mary was naughty.

" *May 28th.*—A Dr. and Mrs. B—— have arrived from Kuala Lebir, having left after a row with Q——, who seems to be a cad. Graham came back to-night unexpectedly, and we all dined together, *plus* Dickson. Had a most amusing evening, as no bridge was played and the tongue had to keep the ball rolling.

" *May 30th.*—Long day at the station, very varied business to settle. Talked to Graham *re* improving the Police. Have allowed the charge *v.* Jemadar to come to a head : hope it will mean the expulsion of these two ruffians.

" *June 2nd.*—Lots of work. Jemadar on the jump again, and very officious. Good tennis, though it looked thundery. We all went down to see a pantomime given by Tungku Sri Indera, the Rajah's son. It lasted till 12, and I was so sleepy I could have gone to bed there. Very monotonous, and the action of the play snail-like ; the scenery varying between the Sultan's Palace at Johore and an unknown street in Paris, the reason for it all being non-existent.

" *June 3rd.*—We all went down to the Siamese theatre that the Judge is running. Stuck it for an hour, but then felt absolutely sick of it and came home. Two nights running of ' native show ' was a bit thick.

" *June 9th.*—Tungkus came up in force, and we

E   49

played badminton. Mr. and Mrs. E—— were there and we all went to dinner. She is rather a nice little Danish woman, pink and white in the plump German style, but the party was rather a frost, as our fair lady could not take a hand in the conversation, which was particularly dazzling.

"*June* 10*th.*—Graham came over after dinner and we played bridge. In the middle Mola Baks came up to report that the China boys had imported some women. They were haled up, and G.'s cook explained that they were there for my *tukang ayer.* The sergeant of guard says they came through saying it was by my orders, and Graham laughingly apologised for spoiling my amours, but really it could not be allowed on the premises.

"*June* 12*th.*—Lots of work. Pen., K., and I played tennis. Afterwards Graham, Pen., and I discussed Guy de Maupassant. As Pen. had never read a word, he did not take much of a hand. Playing bridge there to-night.

"*June* 14*th.*—Pen. and I started at seven and walked to Tupat—very jolly, pretty walk; hot, but a breeze. Borrowed Elster's boat and went out beyond the bar and bathed. Glorious, though the sun was like a burning glass as it was nearly mid-day. Four sturdy Malays rowed us out and in. Tiffined with the Elsters, and were then rowed part of the way back. Finished on foot; bath and tea. Government is going to buy Elster's house, after he leaves next week, as a rest-house, so we shall be able to spend week-ends at sea.

"*June* 17*th.*—Bought my dog 'Jack' off the Jemadar

for five dollars, and brought him home. Ought to be able to train him as I've got him young.

"*June 18th.*—Fearful long day in court dealing with the boot case. Perfectly convinced the story of —— and the Jemadar is a fabrication, and that the Jemadar really sold the boots. My leading questions in court really disconcerted him.

"*June 20th.*—Pen. and I walked down to Kuala, starting at three, and being paddled as far as Kampong Laut. Tried to take Jack, but he absolutely refused to come. Dined with M——, who favoured us with gramophone selections. He ought not to have left his counter, but he means very well. A little difficult when he always calls you "Mr."

"*June 21st.*—Up at five in the half light of dawn, and paddled out to the bar; it seemed miles. Then a glorious hour's sea-bath, a long paddle home, farewell to the Elsters, and a terribly hot walk back, temp. 89°. Half an hour to wait at the ferry, getting in at eleven, clamouring for bath and food.

"*June 22nd.*—A damned hot day, and my prickly heat pretty unpleasant. In cross-examining a police constable who had stolen from another, the power of my glance was so effectively stern that the man fainted and had to be held up. Graham came back. We played tennis, followed by a talk on life and the means and meaning of a happy existence.

"*June 23rd.*—Stroll before breakfast with the dog. Had to tell the Jemadar pretty clearly that I knew the real tale of the boots, and also drop heavily on a private

for laying information against his superior officer. . . .
I think it is almost time we got a chance visitor.

"*June 25th.*—Mail day. Chinese have spoilt the
dog by giving it food, and I had to beat it for refusing
to come a walk with me; and Jack is now very craven
and loth to come near me. Afraid he has not much
spirit. Terrific rain-storm; Mahommedan barracks
completely blown down. Went out on river in a prahu
to watch the sunset—very fine.

"*June 26th.*—Pretty hot day, but cool evening.
Played tennis with Pen. and K. Watched a most
magnificent sunset over the river: rose, and then blood-
red, making the water look as the Midianites must
have seen the trenches (*vide* O.T.). In the evening
read *Toine*, etc., by my old friend Guy; but this book
was a distinctly inferior collection,—graphic it is true,
but uninteresting in every way; none of his accustomed
smartness, and not even very ' French.'

"*July 1st.*—Wore my new white spiked helmet for
first time. Magnificence at expense of comfort. It
has a rotten narrow little brim. Dog made a nuisance
of himself at night. He will have to be chained up.

"*July 15th.*—A great field-day, one civil police-
constable and six Indians being sacked. Graham and
I inspected barracks and new gaol before breakfast.

"*July 18th.*—To-day my orderly said he wanted to
get married, and that, as he was a stranger here, I was
his father and mother. This meant a dower of fifteen
dollars. He is fetching his lady from Tobar. Played
cricket—all of us at the nets. Quite good fun.

" *July* 19*th*.—Jack again tore the table-cloth, and I foresee the purchase of a new one. Graham and I sat talking till 7.30. He told me lots about his life in Burmah, and the row on the frontier he went through, and was awfully interesting.

" *July* 21*st*.—Took Jack a long ramble before breakfast, and saw poor John Nairn's grave.[1] At breakfast got a note from Graham saying Jack had killed another chicken. Thrashed him till I nearly dropped. He must stop it or I shall have to give him back to Jemadar.

" *July* 26*th*.—Jack and I rambled. Graham came in after breakfast, and we wasted half the morning talking. Had a stroll with Stoltz, and his two rough customers came to dine with Graham. One was full of bounce, and the other wrestled with a tough cutlet with his fish-knife. It was quite amusing. I learnt more of tin in a vague way than I ever knew before.

" *July* 27*th*.—We had a huge storm as I was about to leave the office, and I had to leave my shining casque behind and come back in my own Apolline locks. Wrote a sonnet to-day called ' Exile,' and emended and finished a little translation of Heine. I wish I could only get more time. Jack and I had a jolly ramble. We are both getting to look forward to it."

That his duties as Superintendent of Police had their exciting side is shown by the following entries :—

" *September* 11*th*.—Came back from cricket to learn

[1] This, curiously enough, was no relation, but an engineer from Glasgow in the service of the Duff Development Co. Though champion swimmer of the Clyde, he had been accidentally drowned in the Kelantan River. His was the only grave in the cemetery.

of a murder and amok at Kampong Laut. Took a revolver and went over. The murderer was mad, and reported to be in his house. I went in first and explored it. It was really quite thrilling. The people were terrified, shut themselves up, and gave me no help. Examined the corpse, and posted guards to await the fugitive if he returned. Got back at 9 p.m. after a most exciting man-hunt.

"*September* 12th.—Sure enough he came back, and was shot by one of my guards, but not before he had stabbed another man, this time a Malay, with his kris."

I have said that Nairn was fortunate in his chief. In 1909, when Kelantan was transferred from the Siamese to the British suzerainty and Mr. Graham gave place to a new Resident appointed by the British Government, Nairn wrote of his old chief in terms which, if this volume reaches his hands, he will, I think, be glad to read:—

"Graham has gone, to the intense sorrow of everyone, and most of all me, for he was the best chief a man could possibly have, and one of the most delightful men I have ever met, and a real pal despite the difference in our ages. And all this he carried into his official work, and hadn't as much red tape as would make a ribbon for the Legion of Honour. I always felt with him that he saw a thing in the same humorous way I did, and that our tastes ran so far in unison that he would dislike a book I disliked, and so on. In short,

A GARDEN PARTY AT THE RESIDENCY.

GROUP ON THE TENNIS LAWN.

(The names, from left to right, are: H. W. Thomson, P. S. Nairn, Mrs. Thomson, the Resident, Mrs. Graham, C. A. H. Keenlyside, H. E. Pennington.)

he is essentially a man you could live with, and more, would choose to live with."

It would have been tedious to include in these extracts the records, almost daily, of the Grahams' hospitality : rides, tennis parties, dinners. I have left enough to indicate their character. " I fancy there will be no frequent dinners now," Nairn says (again in 1909), " but a formal affair every six months. Of course, with the Grahams, one dined about twice a week at the Residency." And again : " Graham used to entertain almost daily, and the more the merrier." Morning rides before breakfast were an institution. And when the day's business was done and the sun declined, the members of the staff and the two ladies of the Residency, Mrs. Graham and Mrs. Thomson, used to meet on the tennis lawn for tea and play. When the light had faded they would sit round in easy-chairs in the exquisite gloaming (for the tropics have a twilight, though distinct from Europe's) ; and there, while the flying foxes and other winged things of the Eastern dark flew overhead, and the tropic Night, starry-kirtled, throbbing with beauty and mystery, breathed her charm over air and garden, they would smoke and talk till eight o'clock, the dinner-hour, summoned them to the last function of a well-filled day. Mr. Graham was a brilliant conversationalist, and he and Nairn were the principal talkers.

People whose work lies in the crowded cities at home can imagine, but I doubt much whether they can fully realise, the immense value of such social gifts, combined with Mr. Graham's other qualities more obviously requisite for a man of affairs, in a man occupying the principal position among a handful of Europeans, in a place like Kota Bharu.

Nairn's letters at this period show the greatest good spirits. In October 1907 he writes :—

" KOTA BHARU, KELANTAN, VIA SINGAPORE.
" *Friday, October 4th,* 1907.

" MY DEAR RIC,

" The long letters that you have sent me so regularly gave me great pleasure. But it must have been a tax on your time. It is only since I came out here, that I have discovered what an admirable correspondent you can be. However, I suppose there must be a reason for it. Probably you have been to Switzerland again, with the open intention of worshipping the Jungfrau, and the crude issue of some Gallic entanglement; or else you have been displaying more than a healthy interest in sprained ankles at Keswick. I would not mix my metaphors by asserting that you have been casting sheep's eyes in calf-love upon some Hebe in a Victoria Street refectory, but methinks that possibly some blue-eyed damozel in some sweet Surrey village may be responsible for your silence.

" If not, I can only conjecture that your English summer has exhausted your profanity, and reduced you to speechlessness; or that you are incorrigibly lazy, in which case I am apt to think you richly deserve the name of ' ——.'

" Apropos of that refined expression, I suppose you saw that its prime exponent B—— was recently married to the daughter of politicians, motor-cars, town-houses, and race-horses. To quote the expression that Brucie most unjustly applied to me—' Oh, it's infamous that a

56

roué like B—— should enchain the affections of aught
but a pig or a toad!' However, God sends His rain
on the unjust and just alike; and should you meet him,
give him my congratulations—that would be the most
uncoarsest joke of all. How long ago those old breakfast days seem! I like to think that when you at ten
are sauntering on your gilded idle way to Whitehall, I
too, clad in martial pomp, am on my way to grapple
with native crime.

" Ah! this is a fine life and one I would not change
for worlds. In the past months I have been about inspecting out-stations and shooting birds, free as air,
and having a thundering good time. Now the rains are
setting in and our snipe-shooting will begin soon.

"Mrs. Graham has been home and has just come
back. For months we were without a white woman
here. The latest is that Thomson, No. 2 here, who is
at home on leave, has got engaged and is to bring his
spouse out in December. A—— is engaged. In fact
Pen. and I are the only undamaged ones—and you
know about me, old chap.

" As for your parting present of books, I read *Diana*
again with the greatest possible delight; the other two
I have not begun. At present I am battening on a
course of Lever, and the old dramatists, with a few odd
classics thrown in. For God's dear sake write. You
can't think how a fellow appreciates his mail.

" Best respects to Adel,

" Yours ever,

" P. S. N."

Nairn, as Chief of Police, made many excursions through the country inspecting police-stations or sites on which such stations could advantageously be built. For these journeys he used either the Government steam launch, or a dug-out manned by natives, taking with him his Chinese cook and "boy" and his Sikh orderly, and spending the nights either with the headmen of the villages, or, when no village was near, in the boat; or sometimes at the river-side bungalow of one or other of the rubber planters, of whom there were, at that time, no more than half a dozen in the whole State. In this way he was able to familiarise himself with the language and the people, reaping much lore as to their habits and customs and the legends of the past, all of which proved an admirable preparation for the important work which lay ahead of him in the Federated States.

The last words of the letter just quoted touch another fact of the life in far countries, which is not immediately obvious to people at home. Here again I have foreborne to reproduce the weekly entries in his diary, though a perusal of them would be a good prescription for such as, having friends in wild and distant parts of the world, feel the need of a spur to regular and frequent correspondence. "Mail day once more," says the diary on October 29th, "a delightful letter from ——, brimful of good sayings and shrewd criticisms—in his own characteristic vein. This is the sort of letter it does a fellow good to read."

"Very feeble mail. My Kelantan letter just received. Nothing from A——, B——, or any outsider, though C——'s letter not bad.'"

And again: "Mail didn't come in early so I did not

NAIRN WITH HIS SIKHS.

get it till tea-time, and then it was a rotten one. D—— and E—— wrote fair letters, F—— a short one, bill from Little's, and a postcard from G——."

Nairn was certainly the last person who deserved to be treated niggardly in this particular by his friends at home, for he was himself the most delightful and individual of letter writers. Of his powers in that art the justest description is unconsciously embodied in a letter written by him on November 1st, 1907. That which the glamour of friendship moved him to say of another, is true when applied to his own writing. He had, if ever man had, the rare gift of putting *himself* on paper :—

> "KOTA BHARU, KELANTAN,
> "*November 1st*, 1907.

"MY DEAR OLD FRIEND,

"Self-asserted honesty of purpose, and thoroughness, were ever characteristic of you, and the letter I have just received is evidence that you have spent four months in laying one more block of masonry on Hell's broad path, and now I can only congratulate you on the elegance and finish of the work.

"Your modesty and hyper-eulogy of my long-dispatched letter (of which the contents have long faded from my mind into the mists of oblivion) rub shoulders strangely on the same page. For your letter is of the sort that brings joy to the dweller in Mesopotamia and other more easterly parts. A letter is a ' poor thing, but at any rate it is the writer's own,' and to friends who *are* friends even dull words can convey some touches of personality which are instinct with life. I mean— but I am in a tortuous labyrinth—such letters contain

touches of style, certain expressions that stamp and
conjure up the writer—nay more, his very tone and
gesture as he speaks—in a word fill the reader with
his presence. Of such are yours, and very few others :
the rest are the putting of remarks on paper in a more
or less uninteresting and forced manner. There are
very few people who can put *themselves* on paper. It
needs a degree of intimacy and an interesting personality. Lucky is the man who can find and enjoy both.
And so to come back, your letter was the green oasis
in a desert of dull correspondence. It brings you nearer
—but with the last splash of ink leaves you some seven
thousand miles to the west, and places you out of the
sunlight of Kelantan, in the misty gloom and murki-
ness of a London November day. I can only repeat with
you that I would you were here among the crickets, the
fireflies, and stars of a tropical night (such as it is now,
mosquitoes might spoil the harmony—but still ?) lying
on the veranda after dinner (snipe shot this morning)
with lights turned down, and two cheroots glowing in
the darkness, and a delicious ramble through literature,
with our old favourites, Webster and Marlowe, Lucrezia
and Agrippina, Shakespeare, Meredith, and Swinburne—
Ibsen too we have never discussed—Glyn Jones and
Leslie Stephen. But why go on ? Time flies, but none
the faster for anticipating it, and in time I hope we may
yet do this under the mighty shadows of the fells, or
the skies of Norway or Switzerland, or even among the
lights and rumble of the Metropolis—the Mecca of the
homeward-bound.

" Thus far, and I leave you for bath and dinner to follow (the same snipe aforementioned, procured with much toil of leg among flooded fields, and some dexterity of hand among the Nimrods). In the meantime, linger o'er your chop and beer.

" *November 2nd, morning.*—Truly the future is inscrutable. Last night I meant to finish this letter, but a cocoanut planter dropped in to dinner, and also to two hours' bridge. Thus my resolve faded. Now it is pouring, with thunder at intervals, and compound awash. It is perhaps the real beginning of the rains, which are working up now and have been due for some time. Last month we had only $7\frac{1}{2}$ inches rain, later on about $37\frac{1}{2}$. It's damned hard to keep dry then.

" By the bye, you ought to visit this country in the present Islamite month of fasting or ' Paasa.' People are not allowed to eat, drink, or even swallow their saliva between sunrise and sunset. Hence the holier you wish to appear the more blatantly you spit.

" Time speeds merrily on its way, and I am becoming proficient in Malay and Arabic characters. By the bye, in *Shagpat* you should not say ' Wullahai ' but ' W-allāh-ee '— a sort of *me miserum!* or Allah's will be done. The mention of *Shagpat* makes me say that I am now in the midst—the mid-tide of enjoyment—of the *Tragic Comedians*, which pleases me the more as A——, who poses in his own mind as the literary lawgiver of Kota Bharu, confesses it incomprehensible—to him.[1]

---

[1] A—— was not, it is plain, an admirer of Meredith. Nairn notes in his diary : " A—— finds *Shagpat* boring. ' The name Shibli Bagarag is far and away the best thing in the book.' *Mon dieu ! quelle critique !*"

" Lately I have been in for a course of Lever—to my mind a delightful writer, when he keeps to the humorous and farcical side of life, and flees sentiment. He is a pleasant digressor, with fifty good stories and no particular story to tell, and he threads it all together on a silver string of sunny humour and joy in life. Not a great writer, if you like, but the pleasantest of travelling companions.

" Then again, I have re-read Oscar Wilde *in toto*, with a view to a monograph—which is not. He seems at first to dazzle you like a snow mountain in the sun; but, as you come nearer and get to know him better, you can look without dazzlement, realise his achievements as well as his inequalities. He said clever things because he was clever, and he knew it ; but he would sacrifice anything for the sake of effect. That was the keynote of his life, and stamps every page of *De Profundis*.

" Then I have read that immortal classic *Manon Lescaut*, which seems to me less immortal than its reputation. I have re-read Webster's *Malfi*, and battened on Seaman and lighter things.

" Lastly, I have spouted in lyric form myself, in rather less than tropical profusion.

" For myself a shanty is now to be built—but the site is not yet fixed. I am for the river bank with its sunset over the river, and blue outlined hills at dawn. Others are for placing me in what is now a byre, with no view but the back of this house. We shall see : Thomson and his spouse return about Christmas, so things must move soon. My greatest blow was the death of my dog, which I had trained to be my shadow. Five months I had him—and then he was poisoned. *Sic transit gloria !* [1] And now farewell. I see Flecker has a book of verse, *James Flecker*. If good, send it me.

" With kind regards to your people,

" Ever yours,

" P. S. N."

The letters next following, written to a friend on his engagement, I give here partly because of the records they contain in Nairn's own words of certain incidents and aspects of his daily life, but chiefly because they are examples of his peculiar charm as a letter-writer :—

" KOTA BHARU, KELANTAN,
"*August 21st*, 1908.

" My dear poor old silly happy X—(this sounds like Algernon Charles, but is mine own)—and so it has come to this, that I from out the (almost) unassailed fortresses of bachelordom must hail as a coming Benedick him whom once I knew as an admirable Trinculo ! ' Ye're fallin', fallin',' as friend Rudyard has it, and it is the lot of the leal and canty few that are left to applaud the fall, which I do with all the warmth that 93° in the shade can do.

" And yet methinks you are over-sly and a low knave to boot ? Was it seemly that from the cold leaded columns of the *Morning Post* my eye should catch that which doubtless makes the heart of my pal dance and glow like a goblet of sparkling Yvorne ? ' You shall

[1] " Poor Jack died at 5 a.m., and I only got him on June 17th. He was a dear, faithful dog and devoted to me, and I feel his loss dreadfully, though I was prepared for it."—*Diary*, October 20th.

hear monthly from me, though they be short ones '—a remark which was no less ungrammatical than untrue, and happens to occur in your last letter ; but I forgive you this. I now see why you wrote a work called the *Seventh Heaven*, and have no doubt that you are still voyaging in that uncharted and fabulous (observe the cynicism) region. When you feel a shade more terrestrial perhaps you will be able to write me a line. In the meantime try and recover sanity. My sister a fortnight after marriage wrote me a letter which beats all for inanity. I only hope, as an old stager who was once knocked pretty hard, that my friends did not then regard me as a blitherer. But you, dear friend, even in blithering would blither sweetly.

" Having thus got it off my chest, I do congratulate you, old chap, with all my heart, and only wish I was in the same boat to row bow to your stroke. But we poor jungle wallabies can only grow liverishly yellow and greenly jealous. When is it to be ? and of course setting aside that she's the most perfect, etc., I want you to describe her. Being, as you are, inconsistent, I suspect that your avowed deities such as Messalina and Astarte have now been discrowned, and a new altar set up τῇ ἀγνώτῳ θεᾷ—(is that right ?),

" And now, how are you ? It is years and years since you wrote. Everything moves very slowly, and as yet we are unannexed. It almost seems as if we were going to be allowed our independence. I hope so.

" Lately I have read *L'Isle Inconnue* by Pierre de Coulevain, all about England. It is awfully interesting.

" I spent this morning haggling with a baboo from Bangkok selling silk, and finally ruined myself to the tune of $72. They are splendid fun, and it is rather like playing a fish. Time is no object here. Finally I tossed him $72 or $90, and I won. He then remarked : ' I am dead to-day : I speak no lie : I see my God. I lose $13.' Of course we all know about that, but I really think I made a fair bargain, as he was so energetically lugubrious when I won. He also complimented me on my extreme skill in bargaining, as compared with Keenlyside, who said, ' All right, take a pair of scissors and cut it,' and apparently paid about half a dollar a yard more than I did—which shows that I ought to have been a commercial tout or a bagman, having a low nature, for no gentleman chaffers.

" Did I tell you I was now an enthusiastic gardener— really quite keen, can tell a shrub from a gooseberry and all that sort of scientific knowledge ? Well, it's a fact.

" One other—when I get on a nag now, I don't promptly fall off on the other side. So I'm getting on.

" Well, dear old thing, write and tell me all about it— the when, the how, the why, and wherefore ?

" Awaiting a screed,

" Yours till all's blue,

" PHILIP S. NAIRN."

" KOTA BHARU, KELANTAN,
" *September 4th,* 1908.

" DEAR OLD THING,

" Your letter arrived by the next mail, after I had just upset the inky vials of my wrath. As you have thereby somewhat rehabilitated yourself in my eyes, I will content myself by quoting the Roman bard :

' O fortunate puer !'

since it is to be April, when all the world is young, and the spring poets and daffydowndillies spring up in their thousands.

' At mihi non eadem : mihi sunt connubia flocci,'

as the same inspired writer might have said (perhaps more grammatically and less cynically). As I remarked before, I shall be glad to hear from you.

" For myself the world glides on but waggeth not. In such time as I can command, I am making a profound study of the coarser wights of the eighteenth century—such as Fielding and Smollett. But I often wish I could be back in Borrowdale in the *more* (not, as was habitually the case, the less) comfortable chair of Mrs. Honey, listening to you declaiming the death-scene of Desdemona or leading me through the magic wanderings of *Shagpat*.

" As it is, here am I with a cigar and a close tropical night, the ceaseless chirp of crickets, and the distant thumping of drums from some native festival. I think the germ of restlessness was always in me, and I was foredoomed to wander. It evinced itself at Oxford, and precluded my spending quiet evenings with my texts or the specious pages of Clarendon.

" Have you heard aught of M——, W——, P——, *et omnis faex infima* of the past ?

" You will be glad to hear that I still hear regularly from Ireland, and that the best that that unhappy country can produce is not yet disposed of, but I live in dread of one day being called a brother. *Di servent immortales !*

" As you have offered to receive and entertain me in your rustic *pied de terre* for a week-end, I hereby accept the offer and shall prolong the visit to at least a week. So jot it down.

" *J'ai vraiement envie de voir votre amante—elle me semble tout à fait ravissante—ein schönes hüpsches mädchen*—or as they say here, *Allah chantek Skali.*

" I'm afraid the spirit of writing sits not upon my pen, but rather the imp of wistful blather, and so—

" à la bonne heure,

" Ever yours,

" P. S. N."

" Kota Bharu, Kelantan.
" *February 5th*, 1909.

" My Dear X——,

" I am rewarded for the many, brilliant, sparkling letters that I write by a heavy brooding silence on your part. This betokens the approach of the day of execution (I mean exultation). A casual remark in a now remote letter of yours suggests that the date is somewhere in mid-March. I remember wondering why you did not wait for the more appropriate beginning of April—spring, you know, when the young man's fancy— you know the rest.

" You will receive, I trust, in the course of a month from now my tribute to your daring, which I will ask you to accept with the very best wishes—of me to you.

67

Greatly would I wish to be present, to be your *fidus Achates*, and see that you had remembered to put on your necktie, and had the soles of your boots blacked, and had not mislaid the ring. However—' *non cuivis homini contingit adire Corinthum.*'

" (An interlude has just taken place in which I have added to my household goods the auto-comfort chair of the Far East—and I have settled with the heathen Chinee for five pieces of silver. It makes my fifth easy-chair, but it in itself is a dream, or the maker of dreams.)

" My gùvnor will be out here in a fortnight, breaking his journey on the way to Japan. I hear that the treaty is to go through in a month or so from now, but no one knows anything for certain. People have cried ' Wolf' for over a year now.

" If I find a friendly and beneficent Government to deal with, I shall apply for a couple of months' sick-leave and try to run up to Japan, for though there is nothing much the matter with my lungs now, I hope, yet I've not been quite as fit as I should like for my own comfort.

" By the time you get this I shall have started my third year out here, and be within measurable distance of leave.

" Now when you get this, play the unjust steward, and take thy pen, sit down quickly and write. I want to know where is to be the *glitterwoche* and where the rose-embowered cottage with the lilac and sweet-briar hedge. (Let it but be a cottage with a guest-room and space for 6 ft. 3 in.)

" By Jove—no, the purple East is not everything, and there are times when Pimlico and Kentish Town would be paradise to Kota Bharu—let alone a Surrey village.

" Well, the mail is closing, and time draws in.

" This is just a hand-grip, my auld friend, from across the seas, and long life, health, and happiness to you καὶ τῇ ἀγνώτῳ θεᾷ.

" Yours ad inf.,

" P. S. N."

The reference to sick-leave in the letter of February 5th, 1909, must be explained. It was during the rainy season of his first year in Kelantan that Nairn got the illness which, cured at the time, cropped up again a few years later when he was weakened by a long period of over-work, and killed him. All his life up to the time of this illness his health had been not only good but robust. It seems clear, however, that in the rains he underwent a great deal of exposure and, as strong people often do, took very little care of himself.[1] No English doctor was available within sixty miles of Kota Bharu, and for some time the trouble went on without medical attendance. He writes in April 1908 :

" As someone says in Oscar Wilde, ' you are heartless, sir, quite heartless '; for here have I for the last six

[1] Sir Hugh Clifford, K.C.M.G., writing of the Malay Peninsula, says : " To Europeans the climate is found to be relaxing and enervating, but if, in spite of some disinclination for exertion, regular exercise is taken from the beginning and ordinary precautions against chills, especially to the stomach, are adopted, a European has almost as good a chance of remaining in good health in the Peninsula as in Europe. A change of climate, however, is imperatively necessary every five or six years."

months been damned ill, and you spinning out your surreptitious existence in suspicious silence. (I flatter myself that even Swinburne could not have produced so sweetly sibilant a sentence.) However, I do not seek to inquire into your nefarious actions, since you are so reticent, but I would inform you that I have had a racking cough which is only just going away, and the bottom of it all was my right lung. For a long time I did not know anything was wrong, only I thought my cough was beastly persistent; finally, the doctor about six weeks ago sent me down to a specialist at Singapore, and I went with visions of being ordered home or sent to the mountain sanatoria of Java or some other place. However, the Singapore man said that though I had been pretty seedy some time ago, everything was now going on well. It was such a relief to be told that I was not seriously consumptive that, no joking, I jolly near fainted off in the surgery. Now I can honestly say I feel a hundred times better." In August he was " only so-so, not very unwell, but not as fit as I was a year ago. I hope that I shall pull through and get quite strong again, but it is slow work in this climate. However, I like the work and I like the country. It would be an awful wrench now to have to transplant myself." By May 1909 he was able to write : " I saw the doctor in Singapore and he said that I had got over my lung trouble, though of course I was to go slow a bit. I'm most fearfully relieved."

So early as the spring of 1908, as appears from Nairn's letters, annexation was in the air. It had been in the air many years earlier. Before the accession of the present Raja [1] an anti-Siamese faction, who used as a fulcrum for their agitations the ambitions of various commercial interests in the British colony of Singapore, sprang up in Kelantan. This party hoped, says Mr. Graham,[2] "by encouraging colonial desires, to bring about a change, or at least a condition of unrest, out of which it would go hard if its members could not reap advantage for themselves. The insinuations of this party, which was sufficiently powerful even to force the ruler at times to act as its mouthpiece, gave rise to the idea, erroneous but natural to those who judged by outside appearances, that Kelantan as a whole was anxious to exchange the suzerainty of Siam for the protection of England. . . . After several years of uncertainty, during which both England and Siam hung aloof, while even the very form of settled government was lost amid the bickerings and intrigues of the rival parties in the State, a *modus vivendi* was at last arrived at, England formally recognising the suzerainty of Siam, and the two Powers agreeing to certain arrangements concerning future administration, the result of which has been the establishment, in the year 1903, of the present régime, the silencing, for a time at least, of the intriguing element, the restoration of law and order, and the inception of what it is hoped may prove an era of prosperity, to which British trade, now cordially invited by Siam, will largely contribute."

Whatever may have been his opinion later on, when he became a British Colonial official and knew the

[1] Raja in Nairn's day : since then he has assumed the title and dignity of Sultan.

[2] In his book on Kelantan, published in 1907.

F.M.S. service from within, Nairn did not at this time view the prospect of annexation with satisfaction. The change was not, either in his view or in fact, one from foreign to British government. He saw it rather as the end, in Kelantan, of British government of the free-lance type, where the man on the spot could plan and act in his own way, and with wide responsibility, and the advent of another form of British government, less elastic and human, more mechanical, more subject to direction and restraint from headquarters. He foresaw, an ill sight for one of his character and instincts, the exit of the man of affairs and the entrance of the official.

The Treaty of 1909 between Great Britain and Siam was duly completed, providing for the cession by Siam of the suzerain rights enjoyed by it over the four Siamese Malay States of Kelantan, Trengganu, Kedah, and Perlis.

" Graham has gone," writes Nairn on July 30th, 1909, " Thomson is going to Perlis in the north of Kedah as Resident. Keenlyside is chucking the service as soon as he can get out. That only leaves Pen. and myself. We shall be taken on, but at what screw I don't know yet. The F.M.S. is a rotten service, and there are forty passed cadets waiting for a job. If they are going to shove us in at the bottom of them with screw £300 to £350 instead of £400 which I am getting now, I shall probably chuck it and try to get a job out in Bangkok or else go to South America and grow Bovril. . . . I'm writing this on my knee so pardon the dissolute chirography. Also note that my style is pellucid, and untroubled by oaths and blasphemy, so that you might even show it to your mem; though probably, as in all other respects, she so far excels other daughters of Eve as to be devoid of curiosity. . . . I very much hope to get home next summer, but with this infernal business I may be forced to wait six years—damn the F.M.S., they have quite spoilt our Utopia. Nevertheless, fatten the beeves outside your domicile for

" Yours ever,

" P. S. N."

The following letter refers to his father's visit to Kelantan in the spring of 1909. It would be hard to guess which of the two took the more delight in this visit, or looked back to it in later years with the greater happiness. Mr. Nairn, who had just retired from the public service, stayed with his son for ten weeks on this occasion, and was thus enabled to get a real insight into the life of the place and to make friends with his son's colleagues and chief before the change of government and the passing away of the Utopian period.

" HONG KONG CLUB,
" *May* 11*th*, 1909.

" MY DEAR RIC,

" This is the last day I have here, as I go back to Kelantan by Japanese mail to-night.

" My guvnor stayed two and a half months in Kelantan, and when he went on to Japan I got a month's leave to come as far as Hong Kong, stay the inside of a week, and return. I've been staying with Monty Harris, who is soliciting here, with—it seems—considerable success.

But all said and done, I'd rather go back and live in the jungle. Civilisation frightens me, and I'm beginning to feel restless in towns.

" As you've not written to me for some six months—though possibly a letter may be awaiting me, and if so I malign you—I don't know what you're doing in the least.

" I went to Canton yesterday, which is about the most interesting and extraordinary, animated and stinking, apathetic and amazing spot I was ever in.

" But as I don't feel like writing a Murray now—nor drawing you a Crackanthorpian thumbnail sketch—but rather feel like making a big tiffin, having for many minutes felt the pangs of rampant hunger—I just remark it was so.

" I see from the passenger list there is a full boat and it seems crowded with girls, but I fear that in this case ' Miss ' veils no face divine, but rather the uncertain maiden charms of virginal forty.

" Yours ever,

" P. S. N."

In October 1909 he writes :—

" I don't know which of us has an unanswered letter to his credit, but I am egoist enough to feel sure it must be I. I wonder often how you do in dear dingy London, and the little mullion-windowed cottage in Bucks with the climbing roses and honeysuckle. The details may be wrong in every respect, but you grasp my meaning—office drudgery alternated with slippered ease *plus* potnia gune. Ah me!—time does fuge, doesn't it ? I saw in some paper a critique greatly praising the work of one K. H., your brother-in-law—portraits of children at the New Gallery, was it ?—wherein I rejoiced *e tua parte*. I suppose one day when I return lean, yellow, and livery, like Sir Chichester Frayne in *Quex*, with a K.C.M.G. and a peppery cynicism, I shall admire the portraits of your quiverful painted by the eminent academician.

"I am probably going to be taken over into the F.M.S. service, and the matter is in negotiation now. They are, however, inclined to be mean, and I am striving to impress the idea that you can't pay too high a price for a really good official. I think it possible, however, that I shall not get back on leave next year, or at any rate not next May or even any time till August. It all depends whether they behave like gentlemen or swine re pay on leave. Failing that, I shall go up to Japan, but of course I would rather come home, though I've no intention of following you into double harness. Besides, my sister should be home from Sierra Leone in August, and I've not seen her for over five years now.

"We've got a few days' holiday now, as the end of Ramadan is here, the time when Mahommedans come out of training, so to speak, after the fast. I shall be awfully glad, not least because I hate the way they expectorate all over the place by day and debauch by night! The rains are coming on now, and snipe are in again.

"I am learning Hindostani now, and have a moonshee twice daily, the ultimate goal being filthy lucre to the extent of $750 as a bonus. Now that I'm tackling another language, I'm beginning to wonder whether I really know so much Malay as I think I do, and whether I shall pass my exam. in it when asked by the F.M.S. to do so."

The fears for his much desired holiday, expressed here and at the end of the letter of July 30th, were happily not justified by the event. In December 1909 he left Kota Bharu, where he had hitherto been quartered, to take up the post of District Officer at Batu Mengkebang, some sixty miles up the Kelantan River in the interior of the State. In 1910 he sailed for England with six months' leave.

His visit home was much taken up with business. He had received from the Raja of Kelantan, in addition to such equivalent of knighthood as lay within the power of that prince to bestow, a grant of virgin forest suitable for a rubber plantation. But his endeavours to get up a Company to work it met with no success; he was six months too late in bringing his goods to market. Negotiations in connection with this abortive attempt to become a rubber planter occupied much of his time in London, and required attention, by way of correspondence, when he was in the country.

Some weeks spent with his father in quaint little lodgings at Studland near the Dorsetshire coast he enjoyed more than any other part of his leave. There he wrote, some time in July 1910, the following letter :—

"THE ROOKERY, STUDLAND,
"NR. CORFE CASTLE, DORSET.

" O SCABIOSISSIME !

"As I have been granted six months' leave and have now definitely joined the F.M.S. (and alas! shall proceed to some other land than Kelantan) it seems likely that I shall settle down into the status of an Eastern official.

" Wherefore it behoves me to join a London club for the beautification of my card, and the pleasure of my soul in future years.

" Therefore prithee inform me on what terms I can join the New University Club as a colonial member, and whether I can in any cunning way dodge the entrance fee—in the present—or in the future, if so be there is a chance of its being temporarily abandoned for the sake of adding new members.

" This information you will convey *quot celerrime tot optime* to me at Seafield Cottage, Keith, Banffshire, N.B.

" I've been down here a fortnight with the guvnor, and can recommend this place as the most charming seaside village I know : all thatched cottages and green lanes and three and a half miles from a train.

" I go up to London to-morrow and shall spend one night at the Euston Hotel on my way to Scotland. Thence to Ireland towards the end of the month, and sometime in the first week of August to Burnham Beeches. My sister has chartered a motor, so I shall see you then without fail.

" I trust it is well with you—dually—and as regards the wee lassie with the weird Icelandic name.

" Yours *ad inf.*,

" P. S. NAIRN.

" P.S.—I'm writing on my knee."

POEMS, LETTERS, AND MEMORIES

While in England in 1910 he was urged to take up permanently some post at home. His doctor, however, advised against a sedentary indoor life, and certainly nothing could have been more distasteful to Nairn. He had drunk of that Circean cup which men drink of in the East. This, and the germ of restlessness that he felt within him, turned him back, whether in a good or an evil hour, to Malaya. His first post in the F.M.S. service was that of Assistant District Officer at Tampin, a little town in Negri Sembilan, surrounded by padi fields and inhabited chiefly by native Malays — an unusual circumstance in the Federated States, which are thronged with Chinese and Tamils. He left Tampin in 1911 for Kuala Pilah, in the same State, to relieve the District Officer, who was away on sick-leave. Kuala Pilah is a pleasant station, standing on a hill. Nairn was in charge there for a few weeks only, but they covered the time of the coronation of the present King, and he was able to vary his duties by organising the Coronation celebrations in that remote corner of the Empire. Thence he went to Port Dickson, as Supervisor of Customs for the State of Negri Sembilan, a position which involved too much paper work and too little dealing with men, and was little to his liking. Here he cast envious eyes on the house of the District Officer, beautifully placed on a spit running out to sea at the far side of the town from his own quarters—a house which a couple of years later was to be his official residence. From Port Dickson he writes as follows :—

> "PORT DICKSON, NEGRI SEMBILAN, F.M.S.,
> "*August 15th*, 1911.

"OLD FRIEND OF ME YOUTH,

"It hath occurred to me that somewhen during last year, I think a little earlier, I was enjoying your

PROCLAMATION OF KING GEORGE V AT KUALA PILAH.

78]

hospitality, wooing the dream-goddess (I prefer the weaker vessel) in your pink or was it your blue room ? It matters not : the recollection recalls the former, though it may have been yellow and purple—with or without spots. To resume, the fact that I am writing to you is a grave reflection on your own *re infecta*. I may say at the outset that I know you are no longer the flashy but somewhat garish dilettante that you were (that waspy waistcoat has no doubt been consigned to the limbo of holiday eyesores—I trust so), that you have become a somewhat mangy or hair-lacking civilian, a respectable denizen of a respectable domicile in a respectable suburb, that you fight the parson when you meet him, and on Sundays wield the pitchfork : the veritable Adam of your connubial Eden.

" No doubt the crimson rambler has completely shrouded that prospected arbour, and will afford the home-returning Oriental a basis of operations if you put up an attractive damsel.—As I was saying, when the picture of you in shirt-sleeves, knickerbockers, and loud talkative stockings somehow cast this pearl of thought before me, there can be no doubt that you are either more lazy, busy, than I thought you—or most devoted. This last is as it should be, but should not prevent your writing to say how you are ; but I'm afraid you blew the gaff on my friendship by assuring your better half that I got as cross as hell if I got no beer, and then calmly grew idiotic (to the silent anger of your spouse) by consuming three-quarters of it yourself.

" I have twice been District Officer in two places

you have never heard of, and am now Harbour Master and Supervisor of Customs for this State. I concern myself with rubber and tin duties, live in a bungalow by the sea, and have very little to do. I'm longing to get back as D.O. somewhere. I like men and not figures to play with.

" Write a line to say if all goes well with you. How is Mrs. Honey and the rest of 'em ?

" I've made a letter out of most nothing, as the Yankees say—do the same. . . .

" Always yours,

" P. S. N."

In March 1912 he came to Kuala Lumpur, in Selangor, the federal capital of the Federated Malay States, where he took charge for a year, as Acting Superintendent, of the Chandu Opium Monopoly—a responsible and somewhat arduous post. Much to his annoyance, the excellent working knowledge of the Malay language which he had acquired in Kelantan did not deliver him out of the pitfalls of the set literary examination in Malay required by the F.M.S. authorities. He failed in the examination, and forthwith abjured all social amenities and relaxations, burying himself every evening with his books, in the determination to wipe out this reverse. Some months later he passed in Malay with a paper that received a number of marks rarely if ever exceeded in these examinations. For the remaining eight months at Kuala Lumpur he joined clubs, took up golf, went freely to dinners and entertainments, and generally threw himself into the social life of the capital.

In the spring of 1913 Nairn went back to Port Dickson,

Two Scenes on the Straits of Malacca.

this time in a capacity more to his taste than his former post there, namely, as District Officer. Here, for a time, he lived alone in the house on the promontory. He was not, however, without society, his greatest friend near Port Dickson being Mr. Wilde, a man a good many years his senior, who owned a large rubber estate in the neighbourhood. After about six months Mr. A. S. Middleton Best, the Public Works Department Officer, now in the Royal Engineers, came to live with Nairn in his house, and a little later the party was raised to three by the addition of Mr. F. A. Holland, who owned rubber plantations near Port Dickson, and who, tired of living alone, was glad to join housekeeping with Nairn and Best.

Some idea of Nairn's life at this little port on the Straits of Malacca is given by the following letters addressed to his father in the winter of 1913–14 :

" Port Dickson,
" *Thursday, December 18th*, 1913.

" My Dearest Old Dad,

" I am glad to see that you are at last off to sunny Majorca (or, as you seem to prefer to call it, ' Mallorca '). I shouldn't be surprised if you sign yourself ' Henriquez ' or something Spanish for good plain Henry. I am having a slap at the address, and I think I have made out what you wrote ; but if betting am taking no long chances.

" I am giving a little dinner party on the 20th, about ten covers, to meet Miss L—— : two or three ladies, and tennis in the afternoon, and ' Minoru,' a very sporting little race game, to keep us going after dinner. (Of

G   81

course as L—— and I have a ' system,' the idea is to
pay for the dinner.)

" At Christmas I shall just be dining quietly with
Stewart and Hodge and Wilde. I got an invitation to
go to —— for Christmas Day, but was very glad to
be able to refuse without offence. Last year if you
remember I dined at ——, and 'pon my word was never
more bored in all my life.

" On December 23rd there are to be school sports
on the padang here for the children attending the English
school, and the Resident and Mrs. L—— are coming
down to give away the prizes. I suppose it means a
little speech for me.

" We shall have the little club ready by then to
entertain them in ; though it won't be painted. It is
of course very small, but looks rather nice, and I must
try and get a photo taken and send it.

" Rain is still coming when not required, but the
mornings are fine and bright ; the sea as I write is as
smooth as glass, and by the end of the month we should
be out of the rainy season ; and, by Jove, it has been a
record heavy one, never missing some part of a day !

" I read some stories recently by W. B. Maxwell called
Fabulous Fancies. I know you've read them because
I've heard you quoting about the train—' I think I
can ' and ' I thought I could,' etc. Really rather clever
and out of the common, they struck me.

" Have you ever read any Samuel Butler ? I understand he is a sort of as yet barely recognised giant, who
has not come into his own. *Erewhon* and *Erewhon*

Re-visited, etc. Some of his collected essays have just been published by ' Fifield ' and are, according to my *Daily Graphic*, well worth the reading : but to me he is all unknown.

" Thursday is a terrible day to write letters, as it is a Court day, and I never know how long I shall be kept there ; and the half-finished letter you take to the office may never receive its quietus.

" Only a few days to the end of the year, and then we start all over again—*ab ovo usque ad mala*—from annual report to rent collection.

" Next year we shall paint this house and put in electric bells and generally brighten up existence.

" I am glad all seems to be going on well in Belfast despite the alarums and excursions.

" Sorry you could not get a sea-trip all the way from Cardiff ; but I daresay you will put in a week in Paris very pleasantly, though I think the spring is the time for Paris.

" No, I have no official motor-launch, and the car is my own.

" Well, good-bye and much love to you all,

" Your affect.

" PHILIP."

" PORT DICKSON,
" *January 15th*, 1914.

" DEAR OLD DAD,

" How go the Baleares on further acquaintance ? They sound delightful. Mountains, sea, and fresh air— far from the madding crowd—do not for the sake of paltry pelf puff it in a sixpenny for the sake of Ealing and all that ever went with it ! The whole picture of —— pleases me well.

"Sorry you did not enjoy Paris. Paris needs the young year's sun, and the trees on the boulevards just riotously breaking into vivid green, when all the world is gay, and the Spring Song of Mendelssohn is in your heart, if not in the air.

"Everything here is going fairly brightly. The club is booming, and we get a daily influx of visitors. We hope to get the billiard-table up in three weeks.

"One of my dear old friends, 'Monkey' Holland, is coming to live here, and Wilde is probably going to be a visiting agent in the district. Lieutenant Hutchinson, of the R.E. topographical survey, and his wife are here, and generally things are quickening a little in ' Sleepy Hollow.'

"I shall soon be in the thick of my annual reports. I have the Court returns here : 23 committal cases, 495 criminal cases in my own Court, 388 convictions and 83 discharged, and the appeal was dismissed.—Result, no cases for me to hear to-day. I believe in repressive sentences, and I am quite contented with the above result."

The following letter was written after a year's service as District Officer, when Nairn was looking forward to the leave that was fated never to come. He was looking forward to it not so much from the point of view of enjoyment as, far more urgently, because of the demands of his health, already seriously overtaxed (like Jack Barrett's in Kipling's fine and bitter poem) by " attempting two men's duty in that very healthy post."

THE DISTRICT OFFICER'S QUARTERS AT PORT DICKSON.

OF PHILIP SIDNEY NAIRN

"PORT DICKSON, NEGRI SEMBILAN,
"*March 3rd*, 1914.

" MY DEAR RIC,

"What a discontented couple you must be. You have a charming house in the country—roses and honeysuckle and all that sort of thing; I know, because I helped to plant them—and then you go and bury yourselves in the fogs and smokes of dear old dingy London !

"Perhaps that church at the back, in the paddock, with its Sunday morning ' bang ' (call to prayer) did for you ; or possibly the suburb sprang up and choked the country. I don't think I could have stood that church.

"Now, as for me, I am hounded from pillar to post without a ' by your leave ' or nuffink.

"I've been here a year now since I gave up opium, ruling all the sea-board of this State with a firm but just hand.

"I'm really very well off. Lovely house and grounds on the end of a promontory, with sea on three sides, bathing *ad lib.*, and the sea only twenty yards from the house.

"I've blossomed forth into a car—a poor thing but mine own—not much to look at but a devil to go. I rarely drive, though I learnt it for the sake of experience : it bores me stiff ; and I generally peregrinate the district in state, sitting behind with my arms folded and a scowl on my face. You figure me . . . as Wells would have said.

"I'm due for leave at the beginning of September, and I shall get eight months, perhaps a year, on full pay.

85

" I've not been particularly fit for some time, and I am thinking of making a bit of a sea-trip coming home ; going to Java and on to Australia, and having a look at Sydney and Melbourne, and then home via Cape Town. Of course when the time comes I probably shan't do this, as it takes about eight weeks.

" I had a letter from you in which you were praising the gory-ness of Masefield. My sister sent me *Dauber*, which I enjoyed : only thing I've read.

" Out East one doesn't seem to get much time for reading. The early morning (as now) from six onwards would be the best time, but I generally have to be working overtime then for a thankless Government on a totally inadequate stipend. At night after dinner, say about 9.30 to 10 p.m., I can scarcely keep my eyes open, and if I pick up a book am fast asleep in ten minutes.

" I am single-handed in this district, and there is more than enough to do. There used to be an A.D.O. ; when the work doubled the Government took him away, on the principle, I suppose, of increasing the profits and reducing the costs. But it's rather rough, as you can't even take your fourteen days' casual leave in the year. I haven't had a day's leave for the last twenty months.

" I've just got a club started here by superhuman efforts. It's going strong now—billiard-table, and something like eighty members—but it looks rather as if I was going to pay for the table, at the rate people are backing up promises by cheques.

" I contribute from time to time satirical and witty verse to the *Malay Mail*—*the* newspaper of the F.M.S.—

under the *nom-de-plume* of Sunny Jim, a name I got at the Golf Club. (I took up this game with vigour, but down here there's no course.)

" I've still got all my hair, but my teeth are loose and rattle like castanets. I am thin as a rail, and most of my inside—judging by my morning disposition towards all men—must be liver.

" I'll send you some photos along one day. Of course I shall look you up when I'm at home, and shove my legs under your mahogany, but I don't expect to be much in England. I'm going to have a look at Spain, Italy, and the Tyrol, Nuremberg, Munich, and the rest.

" This is all about myself—but what you asked for.

" I salute your πoτνία γυνὴ (I haven't any Greek or Latin left and can't remember whether this means ' fat ' or ' comely '—take it as the last).

" Yours ever,

" P. S. NAIRN."

Time and fate have distilled a mournful irony from the jesting words with which this letter closes. Out of their context, they are like fey words, charged with presage : like the wail of Echo's antiphones in the fifth act of the *Duchess of Malfi*. " Take it as the last." For me, it was the last, of him and his letters.

He was badly overworked and run down. That anything was seriously wrong was never suspected by his friends, nor, so far as is known, by himself, and he had not consulted a doctor. On May 13th he wrote a cheerful letter home, and after the day's work went a motor drive. The same evening he died suddenly from rupture of a blood-vessel on the lungs. He is buried in the churchyard at Seremban, the State capital, some miles inland from Port Dickson. Many friends, colleagues, and subordinates, including the whole of the Clerical and Marine Staffs, attended the procession to Port Dickson station, and there was a very large attendance at the funeral service. " By his untimely death," wrote one who knew him, " his intimates have lost a friend who cannot be replaced, and the Government a brilliant and faithful servant who, if spared, would have filled ably the highest offices."

CHAPTER V

LIFE AND LITERATURE

A LADY who was introduced to Nairn for the first time when he was home on leave in 1910 christened him " the Viking." Whether by chance or by instinct, she spoke a word which touched, more truly than any other label could, the essential elements of his character. For it was not in stature and outward seeming only that he resembled the Northmen. It is among the heroes of the Sagas that you will find, most of all, that combination of the man of action and the poet which was present in Nairn. He was, in spirit, a descendant of such men as that Egil Skallagrim's son, who fought and harried over many seas and kingdoms, and who, falling at York into the hands of his sworn enemy King Eric Blood-axe, so charmed him by a poem of his own making, " of twenty stanzas," that the King let him go in peace. Or that later poet, Thormod Coalbrowskald, wounded to the death at Sticklestead, who with his own hands pulled the arrow from his side, and seeing on the barbs of it sinews from the heart, some red some white, said, " We have been well fed, we King's men : I am fat yet about the heart-roots." English people as a class are slow to realise the value of this combination, which yet produces the finest type of Englishman.

In many respects Nairn was typically English. He

loved all outdoor exercises, all sports and games : he loved also fair-play, justice, and honest dealing. I have known him at Trinity, unsupported in a roomful of hostile witnesses, protest violently against the ragging of some freshman who was deservedly unpopular, and whom he scarcely knew to speak to. One foolish fellow boasted to the sympathetic audience of how he and his friends had smashed the victim's windows. "You did, did you ? " said Nairn. " Do you know what I think of you ? I think you're a white-livered skunk."

Petty deceitfulness roused his anger. " I've got the parson staying with me," he wrote in 1914, " and have just smacked the boy on both cheeks for saying the cat, or the water-carrier, or some such impossible *Deus ex machina* has polished off half the bottle of Burgundy I opened last night, which the parson wants for Communion Service. Now I'm expecting him to give notice. I loathe the liar. If he'd only say ' I pinched it— there was only a little left,' I could be genial to him, and ask him if he liked it."

He possessed the British virtues of phlegm, level-headedness, and freedom from self-consciousness. The genius that presided over his birth preserved him from the defects of these qualities—stolidity, lack of imagination, lack of manners. His sense of humour was strong, kindly, delicate, and comprehensive. But he had also wit, a possession far rarer among our countrymen. Both are illustrated so freely in his letters and verses that I need not waste space in striving to describe what eludes description or analysis. The rainbow lights of comic appreciation and expression show themselves, like the shimmering colours of certain kinds of fishes, only on the living organism.

One little episode may, however, be mentioned here, since it is not recorded in the earlier chapters. A new railway line had been made in Negri Sembilan, and the Manager asked Nairn, in his capacity as District Officer, to christen the station nearest his post. The Manager, who was ignorant of Malay, duly accepted, and caused to be posted up in golden letters on the station, two words in that tongue suggested by Nairn. The name thus emblazoned afforded great joy to those who, unlike the Manager, could understand it, its interpretation being *The Stopping-place of the Snail*. This merry jest caused much laughter in the clubs at Kuala Lumpur.

Greatest and most important of the characteristics which we are proud to think peculiarly British, is one which is largely perhaps the product of those already named : the power of dealing with men and, without bullying or cajolery, of influencing them and steering them in a rational and comprehensible course of life. This power was Nairn's, and it is beyond price for one who has to do with native races, and is engaged in the work of Empire building. " He was respected and liked by the natives," wrote a friend after his death, " and for more solid reasons than mere popularity-seeking leniency ; the general opinion of those natives who at any time had the misfortune to appear before him in court may be freely translated as ' He was a beast, but a just beast.' Although overworked, he was ever ready to give a sympathetic hearing to those in trouble and to spend valuable time in helping them out of their difficulties."

After all, the beginning and the end of it all is expressed in his own saying, " I like men and not figures to play with."   As Meredith's poet declares in *Shagpat*—

The man of men who knoweth men, the Man of men is he !
His army is the human race, and every foe must flee.

His descriptions of people are often vivid and humorous. " Mrs. ——," he says, " is rather a terror—the typical burra mem-sahib, with a bleak stary face like the side of a sky-scraper, and a rasping voice."   Elsewhere he says, " X—— may be a good official, but I think his brain is machine-made.   He probably worked very hard at school, and never got thwacked, and taking a scholarship mugged hard, and never got hauled before a college meeting.   He hates society and never entertains."

Throughout his life, at school and at the 'varsity, in England and abroad, Nairn was popular.   He had the gift of being all things to all men, with the saving graces of a strong will, a loyal and affectionate nature, and a fine scorn of knaves and fools, which made him a rock against those winds and waves of swaying sympathies and opinions by which your good-natured man is apt to be wafted forth and back at random.   Thus, though of wide acquaintance and roving disposition, he was neither facile nor fickle in his friendship.   It is an indication of the bedrock soundness of his character that though a youngest child and only son, no doubt well petted (and also well teased) by four adoring sisters, he never became spoilt.   As is universally the case with people of really sound character, the affection bestowed upon him simply caused the best and worthiest sides of his nature to expand and flourish.

OF PHILIP SIDNEY NAIRN

His early travels abroad, and the acquaintance they gave him with people of other nationalities and other than British ideals, helped to prevent his becoming insular. It was partly due to this, more perhaps to the Sicilian strain in his blood, that he was free from that queer shyness of poetic feeling which makes many Englishmen, of genuine sensibility and appreciation of the beautiful, the pathetic, the sublime in life and in art, maintain an awkward and unilluminating silence on such subjects.

Of literature Nairn showed an early appreciation. His list of books read, with short comments on each, extends without a break from the year 1893, when he was only ten, to April 1914, the last month of his life. He was not precocious in his tastes, nor a prig, so that it is natural that the early entries should represent in the main story-books : from Henty, Ballantyne, and Talbot Baines Reed to Stanley Weyman, Guy Boothby, Marion Crawford, Anstey, and Conan Doyle, with comments such as " ripping," " very much," " exciting : good," " plenty of go," and so on. But even at this stage he had an eye to style. " Very good. Not style," he says of *The Sowers* by H. S. Merriman, and of his *With Edged Tools*, " Good. Style and grammar bad " ; of *That Frenchman* by Archibald Clavering Gunter, " Vast ! but bad English." Of *King John*, the first Shakespeare play noted, read in the Christmas holidays of 1899, he says, with commendable prudence, " I cannot criticise." He had already at this time read and enjoyed *The Heart of Midlothian* and *Anne of*

Geierstein, as well as *With Kitchener to Khartoum* by
G. W. Steevens, of whose books he was always fond.
He enjoys Dumas ; is, oddly enough, bored by parts of
The Moonstone by Wilkie Collins, though he notes it as
" very clever " ; and pronounces Carlyle's *Heroes* " a
necessary evil." In the spring and summer of 1900
he has a great course of Thackeray, destined to be one
of his favourite writers, and Macaulay. Marlowe,
another of his favourites, first appears with his *Edward II*
and *Dr. Faustus* the following Christmas ; Shakespeare,
Scott, and Thackeray (including *Vanity Fair*, *The
Newcomes*, and *Esmond*) come at frequent intervals.
Guy Boothby, an early idol, is shattered early in 1902,
Farewell, Nikola! being dismissed with " Thank God !
Illiterate drivel ! " Many plays of Shakespeare come
up for a second reading ; of Lamb, whose *Essays of
Elia* he read early in 1902, he notes " I dislike his jerky
style." Fitzgerald's *Omar Khayyam*, one of the books
he loved best in later life, was read first in the summer
holidays of 1902. So, it appears, was *Paradise Lost* :
there is no comment, but I think his feelings towards it
were temperate.

This ends his school days. An average of nearly a
book a week during the last three or four years of this
period is not a bad record for a school-boy. Nor is the
considerably higher average of nearly seventy a year,
shown by the remaining entries from 1903 to 1914, a
bad record for a man of busy and active pursuits. At
Oxford he made his first acquaintance with Meredith,
Maupassant, and Swinburne, three of his favourite
authors, also with Sheridan, Jane Austen, Du Maurier,
Webster, Shelley, Kipling, and Oscar Wilde. Among
the books read for the first time in his Oxford days are
Jane Austen's *Emma* and Mrs. Gaskell's *Cranford*, both

of which delighted him by their quiet humour and character drawing; *Gulliver's Travels*; various books by Robert Louis Stevenson; *The Picture of Dorian Gray*; Disraeli's *Endymion*, " clever, interesting, epigrammatic, easy style "; Johnson's *Rasselas*, " dull: arrives at no conclusion: stilted "; *Trilby* and *Peter Ibbetson*, the former read a second time on returning from the Quartier Latin in the Easter vacation of 1904, and found to have a renewed charm; *Wuthering Heights, Jane Eyre, Shirley; John Inglesant*—" Henty! with a big dash of God. How Inglesant would have revelled in twentieth-century cures! " Anthony Hope still keeps his charm, and *The Chronicles of Count Antonio* are " almost as delightful as ' Osra '—but was such an Antonio possible in mediæval Italy? " To these must be added many plays, ancient and modern, Shakespeare, Beaumont and Fletcher, the two great Italian tragedies of Webster, Sheridan's *School for Scandal* and *The Rivals*, Victor Hugo's *Lucrèce Borgia*—" a fine, virile play: the two alternative endings are banal "; Shelley's *Cenci*—" a fine play, and fine poetry; to be read again "; Oscar Wilde, Rostand, Alexandre Dumas *fils*, Stephen Phillips, Henry Arthur Jones, Pinero. As regards poetry, he read a good deal of Swinburne, Shelley, and Tennyson, also Scott, Mrs. Browning, Longfellow's *Hiawatha*, Aytoun's *Lays of the Scottish Cavaliers*, William Watson—" imitation of other poets: rarely original; but musical "—Sir Lewis Morris's *Epic of Hades*, Oscar Wilde's Poems, which on a second reading are pronounced " Tinsel: like eating honey with a spoon," though he notes with approval *The Grave of Shelley, Easter Day*, and *Hélas!* Mrs. Meynell he holds for a miserable poetaster. *Omar Khayyam* appears for the fourth time in the summer of 1905 with

a note, " I have learnt most of it by heart." Many
lighter, as well as heavier and less literary, works I pass
by, but it may be noted that he took great delight in
W. W. Jacobs, and enjoyed Pett Ridge's stories.
Jerome K. Jerome he could not abide, his comments
on one book being " pretty average drivel: cheap
forced humour," and on another (*Three Men in a Boat*),
" over-rated: certainly funny in parts: but I was
disappointed in it—vulgar."

In later years he extended his knowledge of the writers
he knew, and made fresh favourites, notably, Lever,
Fielding, Smollett, and H. G. Wells.

He read nearly all Meredith's novels, returning
particularly to *Diana of the Crossways*, and also to *The
Shaving of Shagpat*, and the short story *The Case of
General Ople and Lady Camper*, with increasing delight.
Evan Harrington was, I think, his first Meredith, one of
the best fitted to serve as an introduction. The only
ones absent from the list are *The Amazing Marriage,
Sandra Belloni, Vittoria*, and (unfortunately, since it is
perhaps the greatest of Meredith's works) *One of Our
Conquerors*. *Diana*, read for the first time in the summer
vacation of 1905, was re-read at Kota Bharu in 1907,
when Nairn says, " It reads almost fresh. And this
time I have got the grip of Chapter I on diaries, which
before was wholly unintelligible." *The Tragic Comedians* he notes as a fine study of the big man and shallow
woman, " a fine study in perversity—the strong brazen
idol whose flaw was clay, and the shallow woman who
would not when she could, and couldn't when she
would." *Rhoda Fleming* is melodrama, but good, with
the " Dickens touch." Of *The Ordeal of Richard Feverel*
he writes in 1908, " Lately have I read Richard Feverel.
What an ass Sir Austin was. One feels that with such

training Richard should have been a thorough prig. The weak point I think is keeping Richard dangling eight months in London, waiting for Sir A., till he is caught by the siren. Any man of his hot temper would have been paying week-enders to his little bit of stuff in the Isle of Wight." *The Egoist* he, for some reason, found disappointing, though engrossing. The last Meredith he finished was, it appears, *Beauchamp's Career*, in October 1913; but he was reading another at the time of his death. The last day of his life, May 12th, 1914, he wrote to his sister, Miss Violet Nairn, " I scarcely read any books nowadays. Always go to sleep after dinner. In fact I am jogging along with a Meredith at the rate of about a page a day, and expect to be still reading it in a year's time."

Of Guy de Maupassant Nairn read at least a dozen volumes while he was up at Oxford, and was captivated by the perfection of his art in the medium of the short story. He began with *Pierre et Jean* early in 1903, but it was two years later that he began reading Maupassant freely, *Contes et Nouvelles*, *Mademoiselle Fifi*, *La Petite Roque*, *Yvette*, *Le Horla*, *Le Père Milon*, *Contes du Jour et de la Nuit*, and many others. The morbid side of Maupassant did not please him : he notes, justly, of the volume containing that superb masterpiece *La Maison Tellier*, that " all the stories are clever, though some disgust." *L'Héritage* he judges to be " a clever but dirty story." Of Flaubert, Maupassant's master, Nairn only read the volume entitled *Trois Contes*, which did not greatly impress him. It is to be wished that he had read *Salammbô*, which he would have admired for the concentrated potentiality and vigour of its style, its dramatic objectivity and detachment, and the artistic splendour of the book, clothed at once with

H　　　　97

beauty and with horror, like some exquisite but deadly beast of the jungle.

Concentration in art was much appreciated by Nairn, and it required strong inducements in the shape of other qualities, such as beauty of style or humorous and whimsical outlook, to make him bear with a book which lacked this character. It is not surprising, therefore, that, while he was always faithful to Stevenson and Jane Austen, thought highly of what he read of Galsworthy, and enjoyed Bernard Shaw, he had little liking for George Eliot, and even Borrow in spite of his many attractions he thought turgidly dull. On *Les Travailleurs de la Mer* his comment is " Titanic dullness." Dickens he cared little for, impatient of his sentimentalism. At *Pickwick*, which he read at Canterbury, he could laugh indeed, but thought its humour out of date. He notes two points in *Martin Chuzzlewit*— hatred of Americans and appreciation of beer. *Sketches by Boz* he found, with few exceptions, barely readable in 1913, and full of false sentimentality. He found *David Copperfield*, however, really enjoyable. Mark Twain, another accepted humorist, Nairn could not away with ; he describes the *Extract from Adam's Diary* as " wholly devoid of humour." *The Golden Butterfly*, by Besant and Rice, was thoroughly enjoyed. In his diary Nairn writes of this book, " Gilead P. Beck is a fine character, though grotesque ; likewise the Twins. What I chiefly enjoy is the allusiveness of their writing. Every page makes you think of some classic or well-known fact. Very well-informed writing."

Charles Lever, Fielding, and Smollett have already been mentioned : he made friends with them in the East — *Jack Hinton, Humphry Clinker, Tom Jones, Amelia, Roderick Random*, and the rest. References to these writers occur in letters quoted in the preceding chapter. W. A. Kinglake, with whose *Eothen* he also became acquainted in the East, in 1909, gave him great delight.

" Curiously enough," he writes, " when your last letter came, we were discussing *Eothen*. I needed no other spur than your praise to read it at once. I had always ascribed it to Kingsley, that detestable prig (who also labels your tobacco), along with *Hypatia*. Really Kinglake is a delightful fellow with a gloriously subtle humour. I felt as if I was taking a delightful journey, where nothing jarred, and then turning a corner or rather the last page, found the path stopped unexpectedly at a precipice, and though eager to proceed, I was obliged to wander back the way I had come, stopping to revisit the places I had most enjoyed. His style captivated me entirely. Has he written aught else ? "

Of modern writers H. G. Wells was much read during his last years, *Tales of Time and Space, Kipps, The Sea Lady*—which he considered " tommy-rot,"—*War in the Air*—" Bert is vastly diverting "—*Ann Veronica, Love and Mr. Lewisham, The New Machiavelli*—of which he says in 1911 " it is long since I've enjoyed a book so much "—*Tono Bungay*, and others. Arnold Bennett's *Anna of the Five Towns* he marks as " drab nonconformity."

Owen Wister's *The Virginian* he much liked : its reading for the second time is recorded almost at the end of the list, in the spring of 1914. Elizabeth Robins,

Robert Hichens, Maurice Hewlett, are read with enjoyment, while old friends like Anthony Hope with his *Dolly Dialogues*, H. S. Merriman, and Conan Doyle's *Brigadier Gerard* remain evergreen.

He came back regularly to Shakespeare and the Elizabethans, and in 1907 (as stated in a letter reproduced on p. 62) turned his attention seriously to Oscar Wilde, meaning to write a monograph on his work. He held *An Ideal Husband* to be the best of Wilde's plays. "His epigrams, when known," he wrote, "seem cheaper." It is noteworthy that the title of *Bacon's Essays* figures no less than three times, at wide intervals, in this record.

If by including this catalogue of books I have incurred the charge of loading a short study with unessential detail devoid of general interest, it has not been through inadvertence. The aim of this study is to set down a record of an interesting and charming personality, and in the case of people of literary tastes there is much to be learnt of their characters by an inspection of their book-shelves.

I now turn from Nairn's literary appreciations to his accomplishments in that kind, and here, alas, we are faced with the aspect of the cut branch.

In his literary as in his official work, he was cut short before achievement had approached for him its high meridian, so that the poems collected in this volume may for the most part be regarded more justly as an earnest of what might have been than as a final expression of his poetical and satirical powers.

The writing of these verses, though done in such odd hours as were free from the demands of business and society, was not regarded by Nairn as a mere relaxation.

He spent much time and serious thought on their composition, revising them with care and with a view, I believe, to future publication. His most successful work is perhaps to be found among the serious poems. It is notable that these, or at any rate the best of them, are all early, several dating from the period before he left England. Pure lyric poetry is in general a creation of youth, and a man's best work of this description is often produced in early manhood. A preponderating number of Swinburne's greatest lyrics, to take a single instance, are to be found in the first series of *Poems and Ballads* and in *Atalanta in Calydon,* both of which were published before he was thirty. *In the Buchheide* (1906), *Exile,* and *Hélas!* (1907) show that Nairn had early reached considerable mastery of the difficult form of the sonnet. Skill in other forms is shown by *Sundown in the Rains, Reverie, To E. R. E.* (*on receiving a certain letter*), *A Fallen Socrates* (1907), and the various triolets. The best of all his poems, in form, music, unity of thought, and balance of emotional expression, is perhaps *Desiderium,* which is dated as early as February 1906. The passion of the middle stanza is led up to by the two first and dies down in the two concluding stanzas with a natural and logical sequence of thought and feeling. There is no forced, commonplace, or loose expression in the poem, nor any phrase that has not its definite place in the artistic scheme. And in the middle stanza at least, there is that quality which may be termed *musical* in a more fundamental way than relates to mere beauty of sound and rhythm: the seizing of what Shakespeare called " the spirit of sense,"—a quality which does not admit of exact analysis, but in which lies the ultimate essence of poetry as distinct from the finest rhetoric.

It seems probable that Nairn to a large extent gave up reading, as well as writing, pure lyric poetry soon after his Oxford days were over. During the seven years of his life in the East no more than seven books of verse are noted, and many of these are light verse rather than serious poetry. This does not of course include Shakespeare and other dramatic writers.

It is not easy to draw a line between whimsical verse of a delicate and fanciful kind such as *A Fallen Socrates* and the lines *To Miss M. H.* and " witty and satirical verse " of the kind contributed by him to the *Malay Mail*, the choicest efforts of which, it is said, circulated by word of mouth among his friends in the East. I greatly regret that a satiric ditty of eight stanzas, to my mind the finest of these, must for the present at least remain unpublished : not because of any impropriety of expression contained in the poem, but because of its character as a lampoon directed against a gentleman still alive and occupying a high position. Much that is delightful will be found in these light verses, though it is inevitable that topical verse full of local allusions should lose something of its bloom when transplanted over seven thousand miles of sea. One or two parodies, notably that of Swinburne embodied in *At Parting*, are successful essays in a not very difficult art ; several epigrams, such as that *For Miss M. Brown*, are excellent. The general impression, however, given by these lighter poems is that Nairn had not yet mastered his medium in such work to anything like the same extent as he had mastered the art which produced *Exile, Hélas!* and *Desiderium*.

There remain the translations, seven in number. All, especially those of Heine's *Ultimus Cursus Vitæ* and *Night* and of Goethe's *Near to my Love* and

Anacreon's Grave, have much beauty. Of their merits as translations I am unable to judge.

If Nairn had not gained full mastery of the technique of satiric and humorous verse, he was hampered by no such disability in expressing himself in prose. There has seldom been a more charming letter-writer. But in judging his prose style from the letters published in the earlier pages of this volume, it must be remembered that they are intimate and personal letters, written sometimes in haste, and always without a thought of their seeing the light in the critical and formal atmosphere of printer's type. However much they gain from this as biographical documents, they must lose from a critical point of view if anyone were so foolish as to apply to them the strict criteria proper to works of considered art. Putting aside, however, such pedantry, a just criticism will find in Nairn's letters evidence of a vigorous, individual, and supple prose style. On every page are instances of felicity of expression, power of imagery and visualisation, aptness of quotation, and in general an ability to put into the written word all the impressions and ideas, all the shades of feeling, of satiric, witty, and humorous fancy, which inhabited his mind. Had he lived to retire on a pension into private life, there can be no doubt that a career both interesting and profitable lay before him in the exercise of his talent in the direction of literature.

And now that the time is come, I cannot end except a little sadly. Though death be a painted terror only, yet division is here, and real enough, and cause enough to be sad. These verses, these old letters, some scattered memories in the minds of friends, with such we are to be content, until we meet—at Philippi. Let it end, then, with a quatrain from his favourite Omar :—

Yon rising Moon that looks for us again—
How oft hereafter will she wax and wane ;
    How oft hereafter rising look for us
Through this same Garden—and for *one* in vain !

POEMS

EXILE

YEA ! some there are who deem it banishment
  To leave some leaden ever-Northern sky
  For this fair scene.   Here months and years pass by
In changeless summer, here the laden scent
Of evening steeps the world in wonderment.
  The moonbeam's splendour on the brimming stream,
  The creak of straining trees, the frightened scream
Of startled birds, the night with mystery pent—
Such things as these can only exiles learn ;
  And if this dreaded exile doth but bring
    As each day dawns, and each sun westward sinks,
    Fresh scrolls of nature's magic, ne'er methinks
  In scorn of such rare gems could Shakespeare sing
" The precious jewel of a home return."

July 27th, 1907.
Pall Mall Magazine.

TO J. C.

Do you recall those days we spent
This summer (ah! how fast they fled),
When chance—or was it Fate's intent
Our lives should cross ?—had made us tread
        One path awhile ?

How, as we moved in our canoe
Gliding beneath the low sun's rays,
I quoted Omar then to you ?
If so—this token of those days
        In friendship keep.

October 31st, 1905.

DESIDERIUM

A YEAR has almost passed ; and still your eyes
Haunt me with ghosts of bygone days that bring
Sad memories, and in my heart the sting
      Of recollection lies.

Ah ! then, when first I met you fancy-free,
The thought that all the women I should meet
In after-years were nothing, passed as fleet
      As shadows o'er the sea.

Ah ! fascination of sweet Irish eyes—
Ah ! utter vanity of human things—
Sorrow, that on the skirts of pleasure clings,
      And weaves grim tragedies !

The cup before me brimming with bright wine
I seized, well-knowing that the wine would please.
But e'en the sweetest cup hath bitter leas :
      So was it then with mine.

The sun of my romance is sinking low ;
Its radiance fades behind the growing hill
Of time : but through the falling darkness still
      I watch the afterglow.

February 1906.

TO E. R. E.

WHO is there who can write one-half so well
      As you, my friend ?
Is it some magic ink that casts a spell
      On words you've penned ?

No !—for within yourself the magic lies ;
      No need to seek
The cause why half a lustrum backward flies :
      You seem to speak,

And I to feel your presence in yon chair,
      Old days reborn :
We talk of books we loved, and books that ne'er
      Escaped our scorn.

No tropic night is here : through London streets
      We swiftly glide.
Hoof-beat and jingle, round the theatres beats
      The pouring tide.

So ever further from to-day I swim
      In mem'ry's stream,
Till, when the writing stops, your voice grows dim,
      And 'tis—a dream.

December 14th, 1907.

TO MISS M. H.

Fair maid, though well-nigh perfect, you possess
One charming fault—a rare forgetfulness—
For you yourself now force me to return
This book you left : so, hoping I shall earn
Your thanks, I send it with the intimation,
" Please hold me always in ' commemoration.' "

June 1906.

IN THE BUCHHEIDE

HERE where the golden shafts of sunlight fall,
  Piercing the forest gloom with dying flame,
  As once the glittering might of heaven came
To illumine Semele through her prison wall—
Here where the beech-trees burn to gold, 'mid all
  The blood-red splendour of their fallen leaves,
  I sit and dream the tales that fancy weaves,
While birds pour forth their sweet-voiced madrigal.
Red, yellow, gold, and rust-brown all are here
  The ever-changing moods of sylvan will—
    Here through the spear-like columns of the glade
    Gleam scarlet rowans 'neath the pines' black shade.
  Ah God ! if only autumn could stand still
With all the ruined glory of the year !

October 28th, 1906.
Pall Mall Magazine.

THE DAWN OF LOVE

How fresh and pure the dawn is !   Silver dew
Touches the sleeping grass with points of light ;
Earth's shrouded beauty waken'd from the night
        Brings thoughts of you.

The circling coronet of deep blue hills
That crown's the gleaming river's distant head,
The stream that ripples o'er its stony bed,
        All nature fills

My heart with recollection.   As I hear
The whispered straining of the bamboo trees,
Sev'n thousand miles of sea, time, distance flees—
        And you are near.

October 24th, 1907.

RETROSPECT

THE months have sped, and months draw on the year
          Since last we met.
Once, though far distant you were always near—
          I saw you yet,

When, with closed dreamy eyes, my whirlwind thought
          Leapt back through space,
I saw you when the dying sunlight caught
          Your upturned face,

I saw you smile (your dimples ne'er demurred
          To play the rogue),
And then—the picture thrilled with life—I heard
          Your Irish brogue.

Now fainter grow the memories that rise ;
          The charm is gone.
But in my heart your memory never dies.
          The days drag on——

                              January 28th, 1907.

A FALLEN SOCRATES

" Who's not a fool at twenty-one
　　Will ne'er be wise, when he is forty "—
I loved to quote this when I'd done
　　Some deed particularly naughty.

I've aged since then, and gnash my teeth
　　(Where wisdom finds no habitation)—
I fear that I shall not bequeath
　　Like Solomon a reputation.

Alas ! though youth's no more a plea,
　　Sneer not, my young friend, nor look haughty.
I rather wonder what *you'll* be,
　　A sage man—or a fool—at forty ?

January 22nd, 1907.

REVERIE

THICK and yet thicker falls the silent snow.
  Here in the dark'ning room I only hear
The ticking of the clock, and in the glow
  Of burning logs I see strange forms appear :
      Strange phantasies !

Stretched in a deep arm-chair I smoke and dream
  Of that strange hidden future, when the sands
Of life run down.   'Tis vain ; my fancies seem
  Chained to the table where as ash-tray stands
      A human skull.

Yes ! ashes fill the place that once held brains,
  But just like mine could ne'er foretell their fate !
So, if some future smoker haply deigns
  To treat in this way my unconscious pate,
      Why should I care ?

January 17th, 1907.

REJECTED VERSE

IF I were Owen Seaman
  With his satiric fame,
I'd pitch into the " freeman "
  Who doesn't feel his shame,
But only lives for cricket
  (Though never plays himself) ;
My gibes would do the trick, it
  Would place him on the shelf.

If I were Rudyard Kipling
  In his renown encased,
The cup of fame I'd sip, ling-
  -ering to catch the taste.
Yet I'd not smirch my glory
  With absent-minded strains.
But that's another story—
  I haven't got the brains.

If I were Stephen Phillips,
  And wrote the blankest verse
That makes his hearers ill ips-
  -o facto : to be terse,
Out-Heroding his Herod,
  I'd call myself a bard,
Stringing lines together odd-
  -ly I'd find far from hard.

I'd sing of England's Darling,
  The garden that I love,
I'd warble of the starling,
  The softly-cooing dove ;

But I should find exhausting
   The hunt for ev'ry rhyme;
If I were Alfred Austin,
   I think I'd grudge the time.

Alas! I am no poet
   Whose words should not be lost.
I'm crumpled up, I know it,
   Or in the basket tossed.
So if (though this were pity)
   The Editor of *Punch*
Rejects with scorn my ditty,
   It will not spoil my lunch.

July 1906.

BLORE'S

(SCHOOL-SONG)

SWELL the song once more and together sing in chorus,
    You who've left the school, and we that still remain,
Praises of the ground, where our fathers played before us,
    Leaving traditions that we've striven to maintain.
Memories return with the words we now are singing :
    Days of wind and rain, and days of autumn sun,
Days with the frozen earth beneath us ringing,
    Games that we rightly lost, games we should have won.

CHORUS

    Here's to the field where we all begin our training,
    Guardian of the memories of fights fought long ago,
    Play the game " all out," for the game is worth the
        gaining ;
    On the ball now, forwards, tackle hard and collar
        low.

Years will come and go, and our days of " rugger "
        ended,
    We shall then recall the days long past away,
Victories we gained and games we lost all blended
    With memories of those who taught us how to play.
Taught us how to play a losing game or winning,
    Made us get to work from the time the whistle blew,
Never let us slack at the finish or beginning,
    Made us play together, not show what each could do.

[1] This refers to the football ground called Blore's Piece, at Canterbury.

119

Things we learnt on Blore's are bound to help us later,
  When the game of life becomes the game we play.
How we played uphill on the field of Alma Mater,
  Learning not to funk and to tackle day by day.
Learning how to play with our head as well as muscle,
  How to use our strength and the way to take defeat,
How to stop a rush when the foe began to hustle,
  Dropping on the ball 'mid kicks and plunging feet.

January 1912.

TO SMUDGE—MY DOG

My little dog, my little dog,—
  Though some there are who ask, " What is it ? "
And laugh to scorn my catalogue
  Of all your canine points, and visit
Daily base vituperation
  On your lack of pedigree,
Showing no appreciation
  Of your eccentricity—

Yet let them laugh. When ancient Britons
  Dressed themselves in suits of blue,
Your forbears chased invading kittens
  Not much more skilfully than you.
Though your legs seem amputated,
  And your body slung between,
Yet fox-terrier-related
  Once, methinks, you *must* have been.

February 12th, 1909.

TO MY GERMAN CLASS

I'VE told you each day, since I came to Stettin,
   A thing that you're always forgetting—
That in England (and everywhere else where I've been)
   The best of us *don't* call it Stettin.

February 2nd, 1907.

TO MRS. HONEY

THERE is a " Green Bank " far away
  From Oxford hurdy-gurdies,
Where peace that reigns the livelong day
  For work to be preferred is.

Whoe'er thou art, whose schools loom great
  Athwart the near horizon,
Come here and work, however late,
  The past spend not thy sighs on.

April 1905.

FOR JESS

My knowledge of the art of verse
   Is, as you see, empirical;
I do not write, to aid my purse,
   Love-songs or ballads lyrical.
So, that my effort is not worse
   Is nothing but a miracle—
Pray critics! let your scorn be terse
   And not too, too satirical.

February 1906.

FOR MISS E. S.

A WISE girl makes her voyage at sea
   A kind of engineering " trip,"
She learns how sudden strains can be
(If she is wise while she's at sea)
In daily electrici—tea !
   So don't neglect this splendid tip,
And make this present voyage at sea
   A kind of engineering " trip."

If I can teach you nothing new,
   You'd better ask an engineer.
I know what pressure means, it's true.
If I can teach you nothing new,
That's what an engineer can do.
Ah ! don't be cross, I beg of you.
If I can teach you nothing new,
   You'd better ask an engineer !

September 1910.

TO PHŒBUS APOLLO

WE long to see your face again,
  If only you will condescend.
Come from behind the mists and rain
(We long to see your face again !)
And pack them off to—call it Spain,
  Or where you will.   But, long-lost friend,
We long to see your face again,
  If only you will condescend.

We should not say the things we do
  If you would only show your face !
And though we only say what's true,
We should not say the things we do,
Because they happen to be too
  Unprintable.   In any case,
We should not say the things we do,
  If you would only show your face !

January 12th, 1913.
Malay Mail.

FOR BARBARA

At logic once I looked askance :
   " Barbara " I hated.
I had loved them both perchance,
   Had I only waited.

May 1910.

FOR MISS E. BROWN

However cold I seem to you
   When now the wind blows chilly,
Although to you I may look blue,
   I'm true-blue willy-nilly.

May 1910.

FOR MISS M. BROWN

ANTIPODEAN spelling seems
In quite a hopeless tangle :
The angel that enchants our dreams
Down there they call an angle.
Oft in my dreams the three Miss Browns
Appear with wings a-spangle ;
They call them in those Queensland towns
The beauteous triangle.

May 1910.

ADVANCE, AUSTRALIA!

THE emu jibbers in the bush,
  The back-blocks echo to the cry,
The ugly gum-trees scarce can push
  Their googly branches on the sly.

The ostrich flits from twig to twig
  Warbling its plaintive pipe of joy,
Now pausing in its swoop to dig
  Its tiny lair with glances coy.

The dingo in the arid waste
  Gyrates insanely on the sward;
Such eccentricity of taste
  This shaggy monster shows when bored.

The wombats wistfully enfold
  Their furry heads beneath their wings,
And, feeling now as good as gold,
  Take from their tails the poisoned stings.

At dawn when bathing in the stream
  The wallaby will yield to none;
His gurgling raptures are a dream
  Delicious as a Sally Lunn.

At eve the furtive kangaroo
  Comes bounding blissful to its couch,
And hastens hungrily to chew
  The cactus kept within its pouch.

The wily aborigine
　　Adroitly hurls the boomerang,
And feeds his puling progeny
　　On platypus and new méringue.

May 1910.
(*In collaboration with Lieut. F. E. B. Haselfoot, R.N.*)

"ALTOGETHER PIFFLE"

(See " Cantuarian," vol. viii. p. 264)

I was walking in " Poet's Corner "
 With slipshod superfluous feet,
Musing madly of flora and fauna,
 Bananas and meadow-sweet,

When I broke into babbly wibbling
 (Heaven knows I was sick that day !),
And the problem I solved was that scribbling
 For us, who could do it, would pay.

Never mind if your verses have meaning,
 (Hasn't Swinburne made music sans sense ?)
Once you're launched, and your bark intervening
 Is printed and heard (no expense)

'Mid O.T.C. news and the doings
 Of those who play " Flieg. Holl." by " Wag.,"
That's the " cardinal " place for my cooings :
 Drop 'em into the Editor's bag.

On the frozen Siberian borders
 Of baking Sierra Leone,
They should vie with the songs, say of Lauder's,
 Sung by Turks to the gay gramophone ;

While the girls of the tribe that's called kissy
   Crowd round and inquire my name,
And some deep-bosomed, white-teethed young missy,
   Black as coal, for a husband will claim

ME—piffle's poet : if present
   " Edd. Cant." only publish this verse,
They may shove in—their job's so unpleasant
   To fill up—as bad or still worse.

August 18th, 1912.

WHY NOT ?

TO-DAY another year begins,
　　And still your heart is fancy-free ;
Why can you not, despite my sins,
　　Confer it, as a gift, on me ?

You said you liked no one so well
　　(I wanted gold, not shining brass);
You bade me wait, and let time tell :
　　I've watched the sands drop through the glass.

Let alchemy now play its part :
　　Time is a touchstone love may try.
To whomsoe'er you give your heart
　　He could not love you more than I.

October 31st, 1911.
Malay Mail.

AT PARTING

(After Swinburne)

For a month and a day she was perfectly sweet to me,
   Danced with me, golfed with me, asked me to dine;
And to see her but pass in the street was a treat to me,
Catching her smile was a day's drink and meat to me,
   Nor did I doubt she was really divine—
      For a month and a day.

For a month and a day I was learning the trick of it,
   Learning to come at her beck and her call;
Though she carried a whip yet I heard not the click of it;
Deaf to advice " I should shortly get sick of it,"
   Blindly I did what I blush to recall—
      For a month and a day.

All at once came the day when she cast me away from
   her,
   Flung me aside like a *stengah* gone flat;
It was bitter at first; but I've learnt how to play from
   her,
Had a good innings—a month and a day—from her;
   Now that I'm out, let some other man bat—
      For a month and a day.

May 24th, 1913.
Malay Mail.

TO THE UNKNOWN GODDESS

A YEAR ago I knew you not,
   When I was member of a mess—
No French cuisine could then be got
(A year ago I knew you not!)
A heathen cook then stirred the pot,
   And stirred my wrath—but I confess
A year ago I knew you not,
   When I was member of a mess.

Each day I worship at your shrine,
   At 9.15 and 7.30.
You trained this Chinese cook (now mine)
(Each day I worship at your shrine),
Chère madame, to be chef divine.
   I never grow what folks call " shirty " ;
Each day I worship at your shrine,
   At 9.15 and 7.30.

February 28th, 1908.

TO J. M. C.

Amid the canes of far Malaya,
　　An erstwhile usher now enjoys
The thought Fate meant him once to play a
　　Lifelong game of whacking boys.

May 1st, 1908.

OFF MALACCA

THE sea breaks gently on the palm-fringed shore :
  No ripple stirs the water : blue it lies,
  Clasping the golden sand. No steamer flies
Its dusky banner, bound for Singapore,
China, Japan. Places that seemed of yore
  Strange beyond dreams, when first our western eyes
  Gazed on rich argosies of merchandise,
Spices and silks and gold, seem strange no more.
The world has cast the old romance away.
Here all is peace. No sail within the bay.
  The blue sea deepens yonder into mauve,
The westering sun has lost its tropic heat,
  And I could dream this were some English cove
Lapped in the summer sun of yesterday.

August 5th, 1911.

SUNDOWN IN THE RAINS

THE dull grey heavens pour their ceaseless stream,
   Unwearied, pitiless : the tempest cries
Its pæan of destruction : the faint gleam
         Of daylight dies.

The shadows deepen : thin white mists of rain,
   The storm's outriders, veil the sobbing land :
The river tosses fiercely : etched in pain
         The black palms stand.

The storm sweeps over, bringing from the shore
   The breaking thunder of the China Sea.
Dark clouds grow sepia.   Sudden night once more
         Grasps Victory.

January 5th, 1908.
Pall Mall Gazette.

TO E. R. E.

(ON NEWS OF HIS ENGAGEMENT)

DOUBLY lustrous, sempiternal
  (As your waistcoat was of old,
Challenging the wasp's external
  Dorsal hues of black and gold),
Is our friendship. Wherefore mainly
Let me moralise urbanely—

May we still as friends be single
  (Doubly though we mean to wed),
And with both " Salamat tinggal,"
  Till the Fates have spun the thread.
That's Malay ; translation I'll endeavour :
The very best of luck for ever !

September 15th, 1908.

140

FRAGMENT

Just as a liner in a blaze of light
  Passes a trawler fishing off the shore,
So did your presence flash upon my sight
  And leave my darkness deeper than before.

March 1906.

TROIS ANS APRES

You came as I pictured you lately,
  As a thousand dreams had foretold;
You trod with a movement as stately
  As a tall Greek goddess of old.

As the sun when the day is dawning,
  So glittered the gold in your hair.
The blue in your eyes was as morning
  Steals seaward through blue depths of air.

The turn of your shoulders enthralled me,
  The glorious poise of your head:
Till your voice from my dreaming called me,
  I scarce knew the words that I said.

Summer called us: you bid me follow
  Where a path through the meadows lay.
We lingered: you sat in a hollow
  Half-hidden from me in the hay.

With hay all around us I pleaded—
  And the scent of the hay was sweet.
The light rain fell softly unheeded,
  For the world was bright at your feet.

I told you (ah! vain the endeavour
  To hide what was madness to say)
The hay was all cut and for ever
  The summer was passing away.

.   .   .   .

The light in your eyes was enshrouded
   In mist as you bade me good-bye,
As a crystal mirror is clouded
   And dimmed by the gentlest sigh.

And I knew, for my heart stopped beating,
   I saw what you meant me to see :
Sometimes you would think of this meeting
   And sorrow a little for me.

August 9th, 1910.

HÉLAS !

OFT have I dreamed my soul was prison-bound,
　Prisoned within the fortress of my mind,
　Wherein, poor struggling captive, dumb and blind
It groped in darkness.　Whirling fancies wound
In ceaseless coils, that no expression found.
　Speech trembled at the doors.　I seemed to find
　The key Earth's sweetest singers left behind,
Whose deathless song repeats its magic sound
As shells the sea-songs that the blue sea hears ;
　Then strength seemed near.　I longed to make one
　　　song
Of such rare haunting beauty, after years
　For this should honour me among the great.
　But when I strive to free the thoughts that throng,
　　I wake :　and all is inarticulate !

December 12th, 1907.

F.M.S. DITTIES

TO MY NEAREST NEIGHBOUR

A GARRULOUS SON OF ADAM

Oh ! China-Chinaman, I pray,
Why am I sad when you are gay ?
You sing the blesséd livelong day,
　You yellow funny fellow.
You dig and delve and plod away
To make your market-garden pay,
And chant your cheery roundelay
　(Or some would say—you bellow !)

I think you see an end in view—
A fixed amount of wealth will do,
And then good-bye to toil and stew,
　To China home you'll hurry.
I never find my meagre screw
Enough to meet the bills when due ;
I've forty years of service too
　Before me : yet why worry ?

Believe me, heathen friend Chinee,
I understand your gaiety,
And would that I could change and be
　Yourself—a shade less yellow.
But as it is, it's rough on me
To hear your bursts of melody
When I am feeling sad : you see
　Why you're a noisome fellow.

August 9th, 1911.

L　　　　　　145

THE POINT OF VIEW

When, as a mere pedestrian,
   I saunter down the Ampang Road,
I find that bumpy thoroughfare
Usurped by men who've got the bare-
   -faced cheek to come and incommode
My stroll by tricks equestrian.

But when a booted cavalier
   I ride, it makes me wild to think
That hooting road-hogs should select
This road ; that monsters dust-befleck'd
   Should be allowed to leave their stink
And cause my steed to prance and rear.

Yet, in *my* 40-horse Belsize
   I loll at ease, as is my wont,
And think police should clear the course
And stop each ricksha man or horse
   I overtake—but since they don't,
I ask you, Sir, to sympathize.

Malay Mail.

MISCHIEVOUS

(" *Mr. Hay, the well-known hunter, has come across the tracks of a herd of mischievous elephants. . . . He is also a reputed shot.*"—*Malay Mail*, May 10th, 1913.)

Aн ! think of the year when I struggled
   Through jungle and thicket and brake !
To stalk the sly Sladang I snuggled
   In swamps for the glory at stake.
My fame is assured, friends' applause is
   Unstinted—that's not in dispute ;
Your paragraph tactlessly causes
   A rift in the lute.

You may mean (the way you express it)
   I'm fancied to be what I'm not ;
You *may* mean—I'm sure none would guess it—
   I'm really an excellent shot.
What matter ? Some comfort I'll borrow
   From France, and a pint of champagne
(Reputed)—my comrade in sorrow
   And insult—I'll drain.

May 19th, 1913.
Malay Mail.

THE VOLUNTEER DANCE

INDEFINITELY POSTPONED

" The Volunteer Dance, which it was proposed to hold in Kuala Lumpur on March 24th, has been indefinitely postponed."

ARE our gallant heroes footsore ?
   Are they indisposed to dance ?
Can it be they want to put more
   Training in e'er they advance
To the conquests that await them
   On the highly-polished floor ?
Cannot beauty animate them ?
   Where's the esprit of the corps ?

Can it be their heads are troubled
   At the thought of too much play ?
Do they want the field-days doubled,
   Camps and drilling every day ?
Till each present non-effective
   Earns his fun by right of toil—
Though he speak with free invective
   Of the hardships of the loyal.

We shall miss, Sir, your dissection
   Of each Damansara frock ;
We shall read of no refection
   Ever rivalling the " Troc." ;
Naught of how the decorations
   On the supper-tables placed,
Like the copious libations,
   Showed the regimental taste.

What can be the hidden meaning
   Of this sudden order " Halt " ?
Were the sergeants over-weening ?
   Are they—or who is ?—at fault ?
Really it's exasperating—
   Why, when all was well arranged,
Mars and Venus ready, waiting,
   Is the plan of action changed ?

February 11th, 1913.
Malay Mail.

"HE SLUMBERED IN CARCOSA'S STEAD"

(" *A Chinese mason, charged with trespass at Carcosa, admitted that he had been sleeping in the Chief Secretary's bed.*"—*Malay Mail*, January 15th.)

He slumbered in Carcosa's stead
   And found his visit passing sweet ;
But thus to air the knightly bed,
   Though friendly meant, was indiscreet.

No dreams of coming trouble marred
   The rest that cost him ne'er a pice.
He knew not fourteen days of hard
   Stone-breaking labour was the price.

January 17th, 1913.
Malay Mail.

METAMORPHOSIS

THE burning rays of eastern heat
  Will turn a temper, just as sweet
    As honey, sour ;
To change the aspect of your cheese
To something that will fail to please
      The sun has power.

Now vinegar allowed to bask
In sunshine will, despite its cask,
      Pluck up its spirit ;
Such is the tale that Bangkok tells
Of sun and heat and Eastern spells
      Or Djinns (I whisper it !)

We know our beers by varied chops
Are haply innocent of hops ;
      We dodge some whiskies ;
But that our nightly *pahits* should be
" Malt vinegar " transformed at sea,
      A brand-new risk is.

April 19th, 1914.

UPON THE TROUBLESOME TIMES

(AFTER HERRICK)

O ! TIMES most dun,
When foolish folk
   Do poke
At volunteers their fun !

In camp and street
We know their worth,
   And mirth
Is surely little meet.

All those who serve
Within the ranks
   Get thanks
Far less than they deserve.

Why force the sort
Who, sunk in sloth,
   Are loth
To do the things they ought ?

No more unnerved
Our hearts would be
   (Ah me !)
If ev'ry freeman served.

But I confess
The latest scheme,
   Or dream,
Won't suit the F.M.S.

June 1913.

THE SEATS OF THE MIGHTY

("*Since leaving the White House last March, ex-President Taft, it is said, has succeeded in reducing his waist-line by 6 inches and his weight by 5 st. 10 lb. He has just given an order to a tailor at New Haven to 'take in a reef' in thirty-five pairs of trousers.*"—Malay Mail, February 12th, 1914.)

Was it lack of the loaves and the fishes
   And Washington's daily supply
Of savoury, succulent dishes
   You felt it your duty to try ?
You can't afford now, Bill, to guzzle—
   You're poor, and you've just got the sack ;
I really don't think it a puzzle
   Your trousers are slack !

Was it Muller, or merely Jujitsu,
   That made you six inches less round ?
You've no pair of breeches that fits you,
   Though thirty-five pairs may be found
In your wardrobe—a job for the tailor
   Instructed to " take in a reef "—
(A phrase from the life of a sailor,
   Who always is brief).

Perhaps it may be that you batten
   On drugs said to lessen the weight,
And a portly circumference flatten ?
   (You've lost five stone ten up to date).
You still may retrieve your finances :
   Just write to the vendors and say,
" The man who's reduced all his pants is
   Bill Taft, U.S.A."

I long, Sir, to see your next issue—
 Perhaps all my theories are wrong,
Why Taft has lost adipose tissue ;
 Your readers may wish to prolong
The discussion—but when I retire
 One day to a cheap London flat,
Shall I remain thin as a wire,
 Or start in with fat ?

February 19th, 1914.
Malay Mail.

DAY-DREAMS OR NIGHTMARE?

(It is proposed to establish a Zoological Collection in the Public Gardens of Kuala Lumpur, and will this collection include tigers and other animals which are likely to make their presence heard by people residing in the neighbourhood?)

An Hon. M.F.C. *loquitur*:

" LET me thank the people who
Want to give K.L. a Zoo ;
   Where to place it is a poser—
   Frankly, Sir, I don't suppose a
   Nice site somewhere near Carcosa
Or in Seven Dials would do ?

" I can fancy how you'd feel
When you heard the wild pig squeal.
   No, Sir,—in the early morning
   When our little day is dawning—
   And it may be, too, is yawning—
Animals would not appeal.

" And to hear the tigers roar
After tiffin would be more
   Than my temper, now angelic,
   Could put up with ; though unbellic-
   -ose am I, without a relic
Of man's early taste for gore.

" Let me cease to be diffuse—
Such a site would be the deuce !
   Sir, I hope you'll not support a
   Scheme of placing in our quarter
   Beasts that Britons love to slaughter—
Thus no day without its use."

July 16th, 1913.
Malay Mail.

FURIOUS DRIVING

("*Two Tamil bullock-cart drivers were each fined $2 for driving their bullock-carts at a dangerous rate through the street at Kuala Lumpur.*"—*Malay Mail.*)

I READ, with something of a start,
    (Though truth than fiction may be stranger !)
That yesterday a bullock-cart
    Was driven to the public danger.

A bullock fast and furious,
    Careering wildly through the traffic—
To satisfy the curious—
    Deserved a notice far more graphic.

I've met—for thus cruel fate decreed—
    Slow-moving oxen in the highway ;
But bullocks with a turn for speed
    Have never yet, alas ! come my way.

The Tamil brandishing his goad,
    Who drives like Jehu through the city,
Is fined—but on a country road
    There's none to see him—more's the pity !

Malay Mail.

STILL THE EVERLASTING "DREAD-NOUGHT"

STILL the everlasting "Dreadnought,"
   Day by day, and week by week!
Rather far would I have said nought,
   But you force me, Sir, to speak.
I and other "constant readers"
Fear to broach your luscious leaders,
For your artless praise of tennis,
   Or the Suffragettes at home,
Lead you to the "German menace,"
   Just as all roads lead to Rome.

Varied and kaleidoscopic
   Is the skill that you display,
Stealthily you've stalked your topic
   Till you've brought me, Sir, to bay.
Why d'you quote the airy vapours
Of the poor dear Fleet Street papers?
Telling us Penang supplies the
   Greater part of this world's tin,
They can never realise the
   Straits that (thanks to you) we're in.

"Cabbage is all right—one plateful,"
   As some old Greek poet saith;
But as daily fare it's hateful,
   And two "goes" will be your death.

Therefore cease to set before us
What (alas!) can only bore us;
Though we all are patriotic
   Let the flood of talk be staunched,
Lest you drive us idiotic
   Long before our ship is launched.

February 8th, 1913.

SOME QUATRAINS FROM THE SELANGOR GOLF CLUB

Now the New Year, reviving old desires,
The golfer in his inmost soul conspires
   How to reduce his handicap ; of this
Absurd idea he very quickly tires.

That record round men set their hearts upon,
Is always due to happen ; and anon,
   Despite the fact they never make it, yet
Their hope of doing so is never gone.

'Tis said this battered Caravanserai,
Where golfers congregate by night and day
   To swallow *sukus* and each others' yarns,
The Sanitary Board will take away.

They say the gambler (out of work) will fly
His kites where Bunker Number One doth lie,
   And disappointed croupiers take the air
Upon the Ninth's declivity near by.

Some men are slow ; but others that I saw
Were just as if a funeral went before.
   Ah ! take your time, and let the others wait,
Nor heed the angry-throated shout of " Fore ! "

And one there is who oft the tale will tell
How never once has he been down in " Hell."
   Imagination is a gift, but—" Pish !
He's a good fellow, and 'twill all be well."

Here on a sabbath morn upon the links
I heard one say, " I had but forty winks
   Last night."—If he's your partner in a " four "
For " Ball-a ball-a ball "—then call for drinks.

The ball no question makes of where it goes,
It strikes the player—and if not—repose :
   But he who bunkered you at Number Two,
He knows about it all—HE knows—HE knows !

Your wretched partner smites and, having smit,
Moves on ; nor all your wingéd words or wit
   Can keep him straight and steady : nor your tears
Wash out the hopeless mess he's made of it.

Then near the sixth he'll say, " I'll tell no lie,
The Spotted Dog, last night, has spoilt my eye.
   But fill me with the old familiar sling,
Methinks I might recover by and bye."

Then said another, " Why in wrath destroy
Your clubs, as naughty children break a toy ? "
   To buy another set at Whiteaway's
Will cost you quite a lot (though cash), my boy.

As under cover of departing day
I sorrowfully homeward went my way,
   I said (once more), " I'll chuck this rotten game "—
I rather think I shan't—perhaps I may.

(Undated.)

TRANSLATIONS

NEAR TO MY LOVE

(AFTER GOETHE)

I THINK of thee, whene'er the sunlit shimmer
    Streams o'er the deep.
I think of thee, when mirrored moonbeams glimmer
    In pools that sleep.

I see thee when far off on some white road
    The dust-clouds play,
When some poor wand'rer faints beneath his load
    At close of day.

I hear thee when the raging waters wreak
    Their sullen will;
The hushed calm of the forest oft I seek
    When all is still.

I am beside thee: though thou art so far,
    Still art thou near.
The sun is sinking, soon will flame each star.
    Would thou wert here.

November 16th, 1906.

NIGHT

(AFTER HEINE)

GOLDEN-FOOTED stars are creeping,
   Treading softly, as in fright
They should wake the earth, that sleeping
   Lies there in the bowl of Night.

Silent stands the woodland breathless,
   Each green leaf a list'ning ear ;
Dreamily the hills lie, deathless,
   Shadowed darkly in the rear.

Speak : who cried ? an echo falling
   Reached my heart from down the dale.
Can it be my loved one calling ?
   Was it but the nightingale ?

February 6th, 1907.
Malay Mail.

LATE SUMMER

(AFTER HEBBEL)

FROM summer's last late rose I breathed the scent:
  Blood-red it flamed, with very life-blood fed;
  But as I went upon my way I said,
" Too near is death, when life is so far spent."

No breath of air disturbed the still hot day,
  Just one white butterfly moved o'er the leas.
  The beat of tiny wings scarce stirred a breeze,
Yet even this it felt—and died away.

February 4th, 1907.

THE ASRA

(AFTER HEINE)

DAILY came the Sultan's daughter
  Forth, and as the dusk descended,
  Wondrous fair her footsteps wended
To the clear stream's plashing water.

Daily here a young slave gaoler
  As the dusk fell came and sought her
  By the clear stream's plashing water.
Daily grew he pale and paler.

And with eager exclamation
  Spake she one night to him turning,
  " Speak thy name : my heart is yearning.
Tell me of thy home and nation."

And the slave replied, " Mahomet
  Is my name, I come from Yemen.
  And with Asras on the day men
Learn to love, death follows from it."

December 21st, 1906.

ANACREON'S GRAVE

(AFTER GOETHE)

HERE where the rose blushes red, where the vines creep
    clasping the laurels,
Here where the crickets chirp, softly the turtledoves
    coo.
Whose is this tomb that the gods have chosen to set
    and to cherish
'Mid all the beauty of life ?   It is Anacreon's grave.

October 27th, 1907.

TO MY ABSENT LOVE

(AFTER GOETHE)

Ah! can it be that I have lost thee?
  Art thou, my loved one, from me flown?
Still can I hear the voice that charmed me:
  Its ev'ry word, its ev'ry tone.

Just as in vain, when day is dawning,
  Some wand'rer scans the liquid air,
Where hidden in the blue of morning
  High o'er his head the lark sings there—

So roves my glance with vain endeavour
  O'er wood and forest, stream and plain;
Through all my songs one theme runs ever:
  Come back, come back to me again!

January 29th, 1909.

ULTIMUS CURSUS VITÆ

(AFTER HEINE)

AH! when life's long course is over
  What last rest-place will be mine?
Neath the palm-trees southern shadow?
  Neath the lindens on the Rhine?

Shall I lie in some far desert
  Buried by a stranger's hand,
Or upon some lonely sea-shore
  Rest in peace amid the sand?

What matters it? God's heaven surely
  Will surround me, there as here.
Stars by night illumine purely
  Death's grim tapers o'er my bier.

July 27th, 1907.

APPENDIX I

NAIRN's record of service in the East, taken from the *Federated Malay States Official Year Book*, is as follows:

PHILIP SIDNEY FLETCHER NAIRN, B.A., Oxon., *b.* December 11th, 1883:

Passed in Law	June 26th, 1912
„ „ Malay	August 21st, 1912
Kelantan, March 10th, 1907 . .	Superintendent of Police
„ December 16th, 1909 .	District Officer, Batu Mengkebang
Federal, September 24th, 1910 .	Cadet, F.M.S.
Negri Sembilan, October 18th, 1910	Assistant District Officer, Tampin
„ „ June 11th, 1911 .	District Officer, Kuala Pilah
„ „ July 10th, 1911 .	Supervisor Customs and Harbour Master, Port Dickson
Federal, March 7th, 1912 . .	Superintendent, Chandu Monopolies, Kuala Lumpur

CLASS 5

Selangor, March 10th, 1913 . .	Acting 2nd Magistrate, Kuala Lumpur
Negri Sembilan, April 18th, 1913 .	District Officer, Coast, Negri Sembilan

APPENDIX II

The following appeared in the *Malay Mail* :—

" THE LATE MR. P. S. F. NAIRN

" An Appreciation

" A friend of the late Mr. P. S. F. Nairn sends us the following appreciation :—

" P. S. F. Nairn, born 11th December, 1883, educated at King's School, Canterbury, and Trinity College, Oxford, came out as a cadet in the Siamese service to Kelantan in 1907. He there held the position of Superintendent of Police, and subsequently that of District Officer, Batu Mengkebang, in Kelantan, until Siam ceded its control to Great Britain.

" After returning from leave he joined the F.M.S. service as a cadet in 1910 and took up the duties of Assistant District Officer, Tampin. He afterwards held the positions of Acting District Officer, Kuala Pilah, Assistant District Officer and Supervisor of Customs, Port Dickson, Superintendent of Chandu Monopoly and Supervisor of Customs, Kuala Lumpur, and latterly that of District Officer, Port Dickson.

" His downright and lovable character attracted to him a wide circle of friends by whom he was held in deep affection and respect, and who prized his friendship the more because he did not suffer fools gladly. He was respected and liked by the natives, and for more solid reasons than mere popularity-seeking leniency ; the general opinion of those natives who at any time had the misfortune to appear before him in court may be freely translated as, ' He was a beast, but a just beast.' Although overworked, he was ever ready to give a sympathetic hearing to those in trouble, and to spend valuable time in helping them out of their difficulties.

"One of his relaxations was poesy, and his cleverness as a producer of light verse was the delight of his friends, among whom his choicest efforts circulated by word of mouth. Other verses appeared from time to time in the local papers over his initials or the not inapt name 'Sunny Jim.' Possibly he was better known by these lighter efforts, but he also published some serious verse of considerable distinction, notably his sonnet on 'Exile,' of which the following quotation needs no excuse:

EXILE

Yea ! some there are who deem it banishment
  To leave some leaden ever-Northern sky
  For this fair scene.   Here months and years pass by
In changeless summer, here the laden scent
Of evening steeps the world in wonderment.
  The moonbeam's splendour on the brimming stream,
  The creak of straining trees, the frightened scream
Of startled birds, the night with mystery pent—
Such things as these can only exiles learn ;
  And if this dreaded exile doth but bring
    As each day dawns, and each sun westward sinks,
    Fresh scrolls of nature's magic, ne'er methinks
  In scorn of such rare gems could Shakespeare sing
"The precious jewel of a home return."

"He was denied that 'precious jewel,' for he died five months before his leave fell due.

"By his untimely death his intimates have lost a friend who cannot be replaced, and the Government a brilliant and faithful servant who, if spared, would have filled ably the highest offices."

Also by E. R. Eddison